HAUNTED INDIANA 2

Mark Marimen

Introduction by
Otis R. Bowen, M.D.

Printed in the United States of America

03   02   01   00   99   5   4   3   2   1

ISBN 1-882376-71-4

Cover photograph courtesy of Indiana Department of Natural Resources
Cover design by Adventures with Nature

Holt, Michigan

Other titles in the Thunder Bay Press *Tales of the Supernatural* series:
   Haunted Indiana
   School Spirits
   Hoosier Hauntings
   Chicagoland Ghosts
   Haunts of the Upper Great Lakes
   Michigan Haunts and Hauntings

CONTENTS

Foreword..v

Acknowledgments...ix

Introduction..x

1. Two Very Different Marion Hauntings.........................1

2. The Ghost of the Missing Aviator.............................16

3. A Trio of School Spirits..33

4. The Spirit of Mercy...47

5. The Historic Haunts of Knox County.........................58

6. The Ghost Story That Never Was.............................72

7. A Historic Haunted Mansion...................................86

8. The World's Largest Ghost Hunt.............................100

9. Two Troublesome Hoosier Poltergeists.....................106

10. Little Girl Lost...120

11. The Spirited Guests of French Lick Springs Resort..........132

Notes 144

Other Books by Mark Marimen

Haunted Indiana
School Spirits Volume 1

Foreword

Late October once again.

It is one of my favorite times of the year. The sky is a brilliant blue, the mornings are crisp, and the nights are deep and restless. Dead leaves crunch under my feet as I take my evening stroll, rattling like skeletons of the summer just passed. On front porches the yellow grins of jack-'o-lanterns spill their light out against the darkness, and cloth witches dangle in windows.

Back home again, I sit tonight in the comfort of my easy chair while my family sleeps innocently elsewhere in the house. The television screen is blissfully dark, and I can vaguely hear the wind as it blows in the trees and murmurs around the house. The fire flickers in the grate (yes, even these suburban gas fireplaces do that on occasion) and the thump I hear from the basement is what I desperately hope is only our ancient furnace rising from its seasonal slumber. The house creaks, and something moves out under the eaves. Squirrels, I tell myself, as I suppress a quick shudder.

In this sort of setting, the ghosts come once more. They filter in through the cracks of the darkness, and stand politely quiet in the shadows like old friends. In fact, old friends they are, having stood silently by on many such a night. And in this moment, as the firelight flickers and the trees creak outside, they are utterly real.

***

"Do you believe in ghosts?"

Since the publication of my first book on Indiana ghostlore, I have been asked that question on a great many occasions, and in truth I have never been quite sure just how to answer.

As Patrick McManus, one of my favorite authors, has written,

"Over the years I have had several encounters with phenomena that

might be ghosts, but urgent business elsewhere required that I depart the premises in haste, and I was therefore unable to conduct a scientific investigation, much to my disappointment." [1]

This could describe my attitude as well. In truth, I have never seen a ghost, nor do I ever care to. Indeed, when asked if I have, I smile and gratefully say "no," and then add that the moment I do will be exactly one second before I vacate the premises at a rate of departure approximating the speed of light. While this answer has no doubt disappointed many a believer in ghostly phenomena, I am sure that my answer regarding my belief in ghosts has left them even less impressed.

For the record, let me say that I consider myself an agnostic with regard to things ghostly. This is to say that while I keep an open mind on such matters, I find myself an "interested questioner." In the sanity of the daylight hours, when I consider the question of ghosts in cold, hard, empirical terms, I am reluctant to give my intellectual consent to such an idea. Part of this reluctance is due to the fact that I have never personally encountered such phenomena, and perhaps partly due to the fact that I simply do not wish to know.

For me, ghosts, by their very nature, are creatures that are meant to exist in the fuzzy netherworld of reality. They dwell in the dark shadows of life, never quite known or quite knowable. No matter how far reaching our intellectual grasp of the world, the possibility of ghosts is always there to remind us that we do not understand all that lies around us. Theirs is the shadow and flicker of the firelight, and the dark questions that haunt us as we drift off to sleep. And, for me, that is where they should remain.

When the day comes that a ghost may be captured, dragged to a laboratory, and analyzed, then ghostlore will lose its enchantment for me. When the moment arrives that the unknowable becomes known, then the fascination of the possibility of ghosts will evaporate like the morning mist, and with it will go some of the mystery and magic of life.

So, on the empirical, scientific level, I will remain an interested agnostic on the reality of ghosts. Yet, on another, somewhat deeper level, I know them to be very real.

On nights like this, when the thunder rolls in the distance, and leaves skitter across the pavement, when shadows creep close and things truly do go bump in the night, then they come. They are as real to me as the mystery of life and death. Delightfully unknowable as the twinkling of starlight or the murmur of the wind, they come and stand politely in the shadows of my imagination. They are not fearful phantoms of Hollywood fame, seeking to wreak bloody vengeance on the living. Indeed, they are old friends, and together we have shared many such a night. For me they are part of the marvel, and romance, and wonder of life itself.

So pull up a chair and get comfortable. In these pages I hope to introduce you to a few old friends. Here are tales from across the length and breadth of our state. It is my hope that these stories will cast their spell around you, as they have around me as I have collected them. Some are old tales, shared and reshared for generations, their magic and power growing with each retelling. Some are new stories of strange things that have been encountered in recent years. These I refer to as "legends in the making." Do I believe them? In an empirical, scientific sense, I gratefully do not know. Yet on nights such as this one, when the fire flickers and the wind murmurs....I hope that they seem as real to you as they do to me.

Welcome.

Note

In the writing of this book, careful attention has been given to collecting legends that in many instances have been told for generations. In some cases, scenes have been recreated in the telling of these old legends that might not reflect historical events. The author makes no claim as to the exact historical authenticity of any of the legends represented in this book. Additionally, some of those who have chosen to tell their stories in this book have requested that their names be changed to protect their privacy. In these cases, an asterisk (*) follows the name the first time it is mentioned.

Dedication

Three years ago I wrote that dedicating one's first book was a daunting task. Today I find that dedicating one's third book is no easier. There are so many people who are worthy of this dedication.

However, I dedicate this book to Bill and Patty Wilkins whose love has not only made this book, but have made my life. You are, simply and truly, the best, and all that I am is a reflection of the love that you have put there.

This book is further dedicated to Jane and Abby, who have taken that life and made it complete. I love you both more than you can know.

Acknowledgments

As trite as it is to say in the literary world, it nonetheless must be said that this book could not have been accomplished without the help of a great many people. Thanks are due to many, but especially....

Patty and Bill Wilkins, who donated countless hours editing this manuscript, as well as providing never ending love and support. *Thank you.* This work belongs to you as much as it does to me

Ms. Loretta Crum, my fearless editor at Thunder Bay. For your patience, your kindness and your friendship... *Thank you*

Ms. Joyce Dudeck, who added her help and kindness to the work, and gave of her love to these pages as she does to all things... *Thank you*

Dr. Douglas Zale, who saved a spot on his bookshelf for this and my other books long before they were book. *Thank you*

Steve Conger, my dear friend who inadvertently helped get this project off the ground.

Those who helped in the research and writing of this book, including the Purdue University Archives and Public information Department, the staff of the Lanier Mansion State Historic Site, The archives department at St. Joseph Hospital, the staff of French Lick Springs Resort, and Mr. Richard King, historian of Knox County. *Thank you all!*

Thanks are also due to Ms. Carrie Flores for digitally enhancing some of the photos for this book, and also to Mrs. Kimberly Chamberlin for posing as my "spook."

Finally, a special word of thanks is due to Dr. Otis Bowen, former governor of Indiana, for showing the kindness of writing my introduction. Having his words adorn my work is a privilege and an honor beyond words.

Introduction

Indiana, carved from the Northwest Territory, is both beautiful and historic. It has produced a President, five Vice Presidents, some of the world's best musicians, inventors, comedians, sports figures and authors – including James Whitcomb Riley who wrote that "the goblins will getcha if you don't watch out."

These prominent figures have helped shape our state's right to claim some part in forming the greatness and diversity of our nation.

Indiana is a combination of many different cultures. We're bound by our local, state and national governments, as well as by our language yet we could almost be viewed as separate kingdoms. From the northwest section of our state, especially Lake and adjoining counties where industry is heavy, to the level farmlands of central Indiana to the beautiful hills of the southern part of the state and from our few big cities to the hundreds of small towns and villages, cultural difference abound.

Each of these areas has its own tales of eerie happenings. It is only natural, then, that our ghost stories would reflect our diversity. Each is different, yet there is a common thread throughout.

The suspicion that ghosts may be around seems to come most often at nighttime, especially when one is alone. The best location is usually in a dark, empty room. Theaters, schools, churches and graveyards are likely sites. Creaking doors, flickering lights, the unexplainable sounds of footsteps, stormy weather, moans and shadows all make for interesting stories and often times convert a non-ghost believer into a staunch supporter of the supernatural.

Personally, I'm not a believer in ghosts but I do enjoy hearing and reading about them. I try to figure out what has caused the unusual happenings, but rarely do I accomplish it.

I'm sure you'll enjoy *Haunted Indiana 2* just as I have. Set your imagination free and let the stories seem real to you as your read them.

– Otis R. Bowen M.D.
Former Governor of Indiana

"He who does not fill his world with phantoms remains alone."

– Antonio Porchia

1
Two Very Different Marion Hauntings
Marion, Indiana

In collecting and reviewing the myriad of ghostly tales from across Indiana, it quickly becomes apparent that ghosts, like the places they are said to inhabit, are each distinct in character. Just as each setting for a ghost story is unique (some set in brooding mansions and others in modern suburban homes), so each ghostly presence itself seems to have its own personality. Some are quiet spirits, content to unobtrusively while away eternity in dusty corners and unused spaces. Others are of a more lively disposition, manifesting themselves in some obvious and even obnoxious ways. Many ghosts whose tales have been told in our state are of a genial, pleasant character, while others are darker and more malevolent in nature.

Cases in point are the tales of two hauntings in Marion, Indiana. While, on the surface, both appear to be classic "haunted house" tales, on closer examination a distinct and telling difference becomes apparent between them. One is the account of an ominous, angry specter unable to find rest, while the other is a tale of a benevolent apparition who became a part of a loving family. While distinct in their tone and character, these tales suggest that the personality differences common among the living may well continue with them after death.

"She was not a happy camper, that is for sure," says Marie Dudeck*, a middle-aged executive now residing in Indianapolis. The "she" to which Ms. Dudeck is referring is the spirit that she says haunted her family's home on Boots Street in Marion, where she lived as a child.

The home itself, she recalls, was a beautiful old Victorian mansion complete with rounded turrets, high ceilings and carved oak doors. Outside, graceful decorative gardens adorned the back and side yards while within, the gentility and splendor of nineteenth-century architecture made the home appear warm and inviting. However, according to Marie, this seemingly cozy residence was also the dwelling place of a mysterious, tragic phantom–a family spirit who had been torn from this life due to a fatal mistake and returned, perhaps yearning for the life and love that had been taken from her.

The two-story house had been the home of Marie's great-grandparents, who had sold their farm on the outskirts of town in the late 1800s and built the refined home in town. By the time Marie's family moved into the home, the first level was the living space for four of Marie's great-aunts and uncles, while the second level was converted into an apartment for Marie, her parents and an older sister. Such a multigenerational family living arrangement, common decades ago, was an amiable one, providing Marie with a sense of connection with her larger family. However, the one thing that marred this pleasant existence was a family connection Marie might not have wanted to make–a connection that seemed to span the grave and defied explanation.

"The first memory I have of something strange in the house was from when I was very little," Marie recounts, "and it was nothing more than a feeling. It was a very strong feeling that I frequently encountered on the staircase." Marie goes on to explain that in order to get to or from her family living quarters on the second floor of the home, she had to walk down a long oak staircase that led to the main floor hallway. Since the light above this staircase was operated by a pull string that was out of the reach of a child of her age, she frequently had to do so in the dark.

"Sometimes it felt very strange on that staircase," Marie remembers. "It was more than just the jitters you get as a child–it was an ominous, cold feeling. Even as a child, I remember feeling the cold and knowing I was not alone on those stairs. It was a frightening, threatening feeling."

While such an impression might be passed off as nothing more than the product of childhood imagination, events soon began to manifest themselves which would not be so easily explained away.

Frequently, just before bedtime, Marie found herself in her parents' bedroom as they prepared for sleep. In time , Marie noticed something odd in her father's nighttime routine. After making sure that he and his family were ready for bed, her father would carefully close the doors to a large closet that stood at the far end of the room, making sure that the doors were secure and latched.

"One night I asked my father why he was so careful about shutting the closet doors," Marie says, " and he told me and my sister that once he had forgotten to close the doors and the ghost of a woman had come out of the closet that night."

Ms. Dudeck says that her father explained that one night, he awoke in the middle of the night and was stunned to see the ghostly form of a woman emerge from the dark confines of the closet and move toward the bed on which he lay. "He said she came out of the closet, pointing her finger in front of her but pointing at nothing he could see," Marie notes. "This was not just a funny little story he made up to scare the kids–Dad obviously believed it and he repeated this story to us often."

As time wore on, other strange manifestations began to be noticed. Several years after moving into the home, the last of her great-aunts moved out of the first floor and Marie and her family took possession the entire home. While her parents retained their bedroom on the second floor, Marie and her sister were moved to a small bedroom in the rear of the first floor that had once served as a servant's room. It was then, after the girls were occupying the downstairs bedchamber that the family began to notice footsteps coming from the second floor hall of the house.

"It was the darndest thing," Marie explains. "Upstairs you would always hear walking but you would go up there and there would be no one there. It was a light tread, like a woman walking back and forth, pacing the upstairs section. Sometimes my mother would call out from the downstairs living room for me to go to bed, thinking that it was me, but I would already be in my bed on the first floor."

Furthermore, it was in her bedroom on the first floor that Marie soon began to feel the now-familiar impression that she was not alone. "It was the same feeling as I had on the stairs," Marie says. "It was a cold, dark, ominous feeling. Most of the time I felt fine in my bedroom. But then, at odd moments, this feeling of a presence would fill the room–an angry, unpleasant presence. It was terrifying. I would be reading in my bed at night and suddenly I would get this sense that there was someone in the room with me. I just knew that the room was suddenly cold and I was freaked out. I was an anxious kid."

It was Marie's older sister who would next have a startling encounter with the phantom. As Marie tells the story, "My sister and I were sleeping in the downstairs bedroom on twin beds. In order to get to the bathroom from that room, you had to go out through the parlor and then into the dining room. One night, when I was about twelve, my sister got up to go to the bathroom and the next thing I knew, she was screaming bloody murder. We all got up to see what had happened and we got her calmed down. Then she told us what she had seen."

"She said that she had walked through the parlor and turned into the dining room on the way to the bathroom when she saw a woman sitting in a chair at the dining room table. My sister was obviously awake because she was up and moving to the bathroom and she distinctly saw the figure of this woman. I can remember that night clearly."

With some difficulty, the family was able to calm their eldest daughter sufficiently to return her to bed, but they were unable to offer any logical explanation for what she had seen.

By now the family clearly realized that they were sharing their home with a ghostly presence. However, Marie had no idea regarding the identity of the spirit. This piece of the puzzle fell into place a year or so after her sister's encounter with the specter.

At the time, Marie, interested in genealogy, began talking to her elderly relatives in an effort to find out more about her family history and particularly about those family members who had lived in the home in which she resided.

"By then, there was just one great-aunt remaining of the original brothers and sisters, so I kept asking her about the family that had lived there," Marie recalls. "I could name my grandparents and all of the nine brothers and sisters. I would ask my great aunt what happened to this brother or that sister. I knew that two of the daughters had died and she told me that the oldest one, Anna, had been hit by a car and killed. But when I asked about the other daughter, Margery, all she would say is that she had died and then no one would say anything more."

The mystery about her great aunt's death was solved, however, the subsequent summer when Marie was visiting distant relatives in Florida. Since the elderly woman and her son with whom she was staying knew the family history well, Marie asked them of the fate of her Great-Aunt Margery. Hearing the question, the son simply replied that Margery had died in the downstairs bedroom from peritonitis. When pressed further as to the reason for her death, the man seemed reluctant to say anything more, but his mother, (whom Marie describes as a "very outspoken woman") revealed to her the family secret.

According to the elderly woman, in the early 1920's, Margery found that she was pregnant with the child of a married man with whom she had shared an illicit love affair. Knowing that the conventions of society would make her an outcast if the pregnancy was discovered, Margery turned to drastic measures. A doctor was found to perform an illegal abortion.

It is unclear exactly when this ill-fated procedure was performed, but its tragic results became a jaded part of the family history. During the operation something went terribly wrong, resulting in a massive infection. "According to what I was told," Marie remembers, "Margery died in her bed in the downstairs bedroom, screaming that God would never forgive her for what she had done."

Marie believes that it was Margery's spirit that was manifesting itself in the home of her childhood, perhaps hungering for the life that had been taken from her, wrapped in the anger and frustration of her cruel fate.

In any case, when Marie returned home from her visit to Florida, the manifestations continued. Then, not long after Marie discovered the terrible secret, she came into direct contact with the spirit of her great-aunt.

"My sister and I were sleeping in a downstairs bed," Marie remembers, "and I woke up in the middle of the night to see a strange woman standing at the foot of my bed staring at me. I could see her clearly. She wore a long Victorian dress and her hair was done up on her head in a bun. She was not smiling or frowning, but she was just staring down at me."

"At first I thought that I was dreaming, so I closed my eyes and bit my lip as hard as I could to wake myself up. But when I opened my eyes she was still there. Then I started screaming." Hearing her scream, Marie's sister sat upright in her bed and the specter faded into the night air.

Gratefully, this would be the last that Marie would see of her ghostly roommate. Yet as years passed, the spirit continued to make its presence known by various means, particularly through the sound of phantom footsteps moving through the upstairs level of the house. It is interesting to note that apparently these footsteps continued even after the house was sold some time ago.

"My family sold the house years ago," Marie says, "and it was purchased by a neighbor. He converted the house into two apartments, one on the main floor and another on the second floor. A few years later I returned to the house to take pictures of the exterior and I spoke with the new owner. He said to me, 'Boy, you know this house is funny–it is a strange place.' When I asked him what he meant, he said, 'There is someone walking around upstairs. The downstairs tenant called me to ask when I had rented the upstairs apartment because he heard someone walking around up there, but I have never been able to rent the upstairs apartment.' I guess Margery is still hanging around."

Today Marie Dudeck seems to bear no emotional scars from her terrifying experiences as a child. However, the memories do remain with her. "It was her house and she was everywhere in it," Marie remarks. "It was not a pleasant thing at all. I felt like she was extremely angry. I could feel it–she was not a happy camper. Not a pleasant haunting at all."

* * *

The unearthly events at the old Victorian mansion on Boots Street seem to have been anything but a happy haunting. However, this is in direct contrast to another old tale of a haunting in Marion told by a cheerful, gracious woman named Emily Kertes.

Ms. Kertes, now in her mid-seventies, lives in a retirement home near Indianapolis. Though small of stature and slight of build, Emily possesses an energy and clarity of memory that belie her age. Cheerfully sitting in the lounge of her retirement village, Ms. Kertes frequently regales visitors with charming tales of life in Indiana in the early 1930s, but her most fascinating memories are of a more recent vintage. These are tales of a charming spirit with whom she and her family shared a dwelling. Unlike the spirit of Boots Street, hers was a benevolent, even loving ghost who once came to the aid of her family when they needed her.

"I was in my late teens when I married," Ms. Kertes begins, a wisp of fond nostalgia creeping into her voice. "And we had two girls by the time we moved to Marion in the late fifties. My husband, Les, was a salesman for a fertilizer company and we were moved to Marion so that he could take over this district for his company. Marion was a beautiful place to live–it still felt like a small town even though it was starting to grow even then."

"We bought a house about a block from downtown. It was an old place, built about the turn of the century. Even now I can remember going to look at the house after Les had picked it out and when I walked in the front door I said to Les, 'This is a wonderful place–I am just going to love it here!' It had that kind of a feeling–a gentle, loving atmosphere. I knew the first time I walked in that Les and I and our girls would be safe and happy there."

Safe indeed they were, as well as happy, for the twenty years the family would live in the home. Perhaps, as Emily believes, part of their happiness was due to a gentle spirit that seemed to linger there.

"The first thing we noticed," Emily recalls, warming to her story, "was the smell of coffee. Les was always a big coffee drinker. He would get up first thing in the morning and go downstairs to plug in the coffee pot–he said he could not think until he had his first cup of coffee.

"We had been in the house for about a month when one morning Les nudged me awake and said, 'Did you go downstairs and start the coffee?' I was still half asleep but I told him that I had been sleeping. Then he said 'Well, someone did because I can smell coffee!' I thought he was dreaming but as I sat up, I realized I could smell it too. Our girls were only toddlers at the time - my oldest was just four when me moved in, so I knew they could not have gone downstairs and plugged in the pot. Yet the smell of coffee brewing was strong."

Puzzled, Emily and her husband rose from bed to go downstairs. There they found the coffee pot cold and unplugged, yet the room was filled with the fragrant aroma of freshly brewed coffee.

"It sure was strange," Emily recalls, "but it became a regular thing. Les would get up for work and the kitchen would be filled with the smell of coffee. Sometimes there would be the smell of freshly baked bread, too. We could not explain it, but it was a nice smell to wake up to so Les and I just kind of did not question it and went on with life."

Soon, however, things began to occur that did make Emily begin to question what was going on in the house. Significantly, the new phenomena began with Emily's oldest daughter, Kimberly. "Kim was four at the time," Emily remembers with a smile, "and she was a little insecure about moving to a new house, so we put her in the bedroom next to ours. The first few nights in the house she got scared in her room and so we took her to bed with us, but after about a week, she settled down and started sleeping well. Still, I would get up a couple of times a night and check on her and our youngest daughter Kate."

However, as the days in their new home turned to months, Emily became aware of a puzzling aspect of her nighttime visits to her daughter's room. "Kim was always what we called an athletic sleeper," Emily chuckles. "She would toss and roll in her sleep and her blankets always ended up in a bunch in the middle of the bed. I would have to go in and replace her blankets. But after a couple of months in the house, I found that when I went into Kim's room at night, her blankets would all be replaced around her and smoothed over.

How the "spectral nanny" might have looked to Emily Kertes of Marion, Indiana.

Photo: Mike Pilla. Digitally enhanced by Carrie Flores

"At first I just thought that she was not tossing and turning so much, but then one night, on the way to bed, I looked in at her and found that her blankets were all bunched up. I was going to replace them but just at the moment, I heard Kate crying from her crib in the next room. I went to change her diaper and then when she was back asleep, I returned to Kim's room. When I did, I found the blankets had been carefully replaced and turned down at the top, away from her face. The blankets were perfectly smoothed, like they had just been placed there."

Somewhat shaken by the odd occurrence, Emily decided not to mention the incident to her husband out of fear that he would think her "a hysterical mother." However, Emily did maintain her nightly visits to check on her daughters and during those visits she would occasionally encounter inexplicable things. One night as Emily entered the nursery of her youngest child, Kate, she caught a glimpse of a movement in the far side of the room next to the child's crib. "When I walked into the room that night, I saw something move," Emily remembers. "It was just like a shadow moved by the corner of her crib–a tall shadow, person-sized. Then it was gone. I ran over to Kate but she was sleeping peacefully. But somehow I felt that I was not alone in the room."

Even more dramatic was the incident that occurred one night a few months later. Walking down the hall toward the nursery to check on Kate, Emily became conscious of the sound of a soft humming coming from the room. "It was soft and peaceful sounding," Emily remembers. "I could not really hear a tune, but it was a pretty sound. I was more curious than scared and when I went into the room, Kate was sleeping and the room was empty. However, in the dim room I could see that the rocking chair in the corner of the room was rocking back and forth like someone had just gotten up off of it."

Curiously, though Emily might naturally have been frightened by such a sight, she was not. "I know this sounds crazy," she says, "Looking back at it I should have been scared to death but I just got used to it. It was not a bad feeling at all - kind of a gentle warmth that was in the room. Nothing threatening at all. Then I began to notice the other smell.

"It smelled like a perfume. I never wore perfume at the time but I knew a lot of ladies who did and this did not smell like anything that my friends had worn. It was sort of like an old perfume my mother used to wear–a little like lilacs but not quite." Emily reports that she frequently encountered this odd yet pleasant scent in either or both of her children's bedrooms as she checked on them late at night.

The nursery would not be the only location in the house where Emily would catch the scent of this antique perfume. On at least one memorable occasion, she also smelled it in her kitchen.

"I remember the day very clearly," Emily recalls, "because it was Kimberly's first day of kindergarten. That is a tough moment for many mothers–seeing your child leave for the first time. That day, we did all the family things you do on the first day of school. We got her up early, packed her a lunch and took a couple of pictures of her in her new dress. Then I walked her out to the curb and waited with her for the school bus. At that point I think I was more upset than she was.

"After the bus came and I had put her on it, I went back to the house, poured myself a cup of coffee and sat down at the kitchen table to smoke a cigarette. The baby was still asleep upstairs and the house was quiet and I sat there thinking about my daughters and worrying about how Kimberly was going to do on her first day.

"Suddenly, from quite close, over my left shoulder, I heard a woman's sigh. It was right over my shoulder, almost in my ear and when I spun around no one was there. Then suddenly this smell of the old perfume filled the room. At that moment I knew for sure there was a spirit in the house and somehow I knew that it was a mother. I was not scared, but instead it was a comfortable feeling. It was like someone understood what I was going through."

An interesting note to the story of the phantom smell in the nursery is that Emily reports that many years later she did indeed smell another scent like the one she had frequently encountered in her home. As she tells the story, years after they had moved from their Marion home, she was shopping in an antique store in Indianapolis when she suddenly smelled the same fragrance in the air around her. Immediately recognizing it, she went to the owner of the shop and asked him the origin on the smell. "Oh, I just opened an old bottle of perfume that I found in the drawer of a dresser we just bought." Handing her the bottle, Emily found a weathered glass container, labeled with a name she did not recognize. Looking closer, she saw a small date on the bottom–1898.

Over the years Emily seems to have developed a sort of gentle communion with whatever spirit was living in her home. Instead of being uneasy with the presence in the house, Emily and her family seemed to feel at peace with their unseen guest.

In return, the spirit seemed to only wish to be helpful. At least once, it even displayed a propensity for housework. "I remember one Saturday," Emily recalls, "the girls had been outside playing all afternoon. The rule in our home was that you did not play till your room was picked up, but naturally, when I had gone upstairs earlier that afternoon, Kate's room had been a mess. Toys were scattered across the room, books laying on the bed - the usual kid mess. When the girls came in that afternoon I read them the riot act and told them to go upstairs and not to come down till their rooms were cleaned.

"Grudgingly, they went upstairs, but in a minute Kate came down wide-eyed. She told me that her room *was* cleaned. I asked her how she had done it so quickly and she swore to me that everything was neat when she got there. Of course I did not believe her, but I went upstairs and sure enough, both rooms were picked up and straightened.

"I was shocked and I asked the girls again how they had done it so fast. Kate looked up at me and said, 'Mommy, if you didn't do it, then maybe the lady did.' 'What lady?' I said, already suspecting that I knew the answer. 'You know, Mom,' she said, 'the nice lady who comes into my room at night sometimes and sings me to sleep. She is nice and I love her.' It was then that I realized that I was not the only one who had been feeling her presence."

Indeed, Emily's oldest daughter, Kimberly, now a teacher in Indianapolis, reports today that she does recall vague memories of a kind lady coming into her room late at night. "It is hard to remember exact details, but I know she had on a long dress and was very pretty. It was a comfortable, rather than scary feeling. I remember her leaning over my bed and smiling at me as I drifted off to sleep," Kimberly says.

To be sure, the apparition seemed to have an affinity for the two girls in the home. The feeling of her presence only intensified three years after the Kertes family had moved to the home, when Emily gave birth to a third daughter. After young Kate had been moved to share a bedroom with her older sister and the new baby had taken up residence in the nursery, the comfort of her presence in the baby's room was frequently felt. Indeed, it was at this time that Emily caught her first and only sight of the ghost.

"It was about six months after I had bought the baby home," Emily remembers, "and Rachel, the baby, had a bad cough. I'm sure now that it was just one of those common colds babies get, but at the time it was a big deal for me. It was a deep rumbling cough and she could not sleep well or even eat much. For three days, I was up every hour checking on her and giving her the medicine that the doctor had prescribed. I was exhausted."

"The third night I awoke at about three A.M. to check on Rachel and as I walked down the hall, I realized that she was not coughing. I was half relieved and half fearful but as I walked into the room and my eyes adjusted to the night light, I clearly saw the figure of a woman bending over the crib. I was startled and I stopped short and kind of gasped and when I did, she stood upright, turned toward me and smiled. Then she was just sort of gone. I went to check the baby and she was fine. As a matter of fact, she recovered pretty quickly after that."

Emily describes the apparition as a woman in her thirties, wearing an old-fashioned long dress with long brown hair that curled around her shoulders. The years that have since passed do not seem to have clouded her memory of that night and Emily vividly remembers that the woman's face "was one of the kindest, sweetest faces I had ever seen."

A clue to the identity of the phantom houseguest came a year or so later, when Emily was visiting with a neighbor. "I had tried to figure out who our spirit was" she recalls, "and I had talked to all the neighbors but none of them knew the history of the house. Finally one day a neighbor had me over for coffee and she told me that her uncle, from whom they had bought the house, was visiting with them from out of town."

"I met him and he was a nice enough old gentleman. We had talked for about fifteen minutes and he started telling me stories about what the neighborhood had been like in the early 1900s. Then it occurred to me to ask about the former owners of our home. He told me that the house had changed hands four or five times in the time he lived in his home."

"When I asked him if anyone had died in the house he gave me a queer look and then admitted that a woman had in fact died there. She was the wife of one of the owners and the mother of several small children. She had died of diphtheria when she was about thirty-five. Then he added that he had known the family and that the woman had been one of the sweetest ladies he had ever met. He also said she was totally devoted to her husband and family. That explained it for me."

Perhaps as Emily believes, this story did indeed bear some significance on the phenomena occurring in the Kertes' home. Whoever or whatever it was that shared their dwelling with them, however, became a welcome part of the family's life there. "She became like a part of the family," Emily says fondly. "We used to joke around and talk to her. Sometimes when I was alone in the house during the day I would talk out loud to her and get the feeling she heard me. Anyone would have thought I was nuts if they had heard me.

"She had her mischievous side too I think," Emily adds. "She did not seem to like my husband smoking in the living room. One night, Les had left an unopened package of cigarettes on the end table in the living room and when we went downstairs the next day the package had been crushed underneath the leg of the couch. Someone had picked up the couch and put the package under the leg.

"Another time we had guests for the evening and we had entertained them in the living room. Les was smoking like he usually did and when they left we cleaned up and went upstairs for bed. As it turned out, he had forgotten to empty the ash tray from the living room though and when we got upstairs to our bedroom we found the ashtray upside down on his pillow with the ashes all over his side of the bed. There was no way that anyone could have taken the ash tray up there. After that, Les got the point and made sure he cleaned up the ash tray when he was done smoking in the living room."

As incredible as such occurrences might seem, in talking with Emily, one cannot escape the feeling that such events were common place in the home. "So many things happened there that I cannot begin to remember them all," Emily reflects.

One incident, however, stands especially clearly in her memory. "This I can never forget," Emily says. "It was 1965 and Les and I were having the wiring redone in the house. The wiring was way out of date and we were afraid it would be a fire hazard. I guess that is ironic because of what ended up happening in the home..."

Emily goes on to relate that one night midway through the rewiring process, she and her husband were awakened at about two A.M. by the sound of pounding on their bedroom door. "This was not a child knocking," she remembers. "It was a loud insistent pounding. Les got up to open the door, but when he opened it no one was there. He stood there for just a second and then turned around and said 'Emily get up, I think we have a fire.' "

Frightened, Emily jumped from the bed and raced to the hall where she encountered thick black smoke creeping down from the ceiling. "My first thought, of course, was the children," she says, "so Les and I ran down the hall to the girls' rooms. I was scared, but I got more scared when I went in to the first bedroom–Rachel's–and found that she was not in her bed. I looked around the room but I could not find her. I screamed for Les and in a second, he came to the door and said that Kate and Kimberly were not in their rooms either."

"Both of us just about panicked right then. We were coughing and trying to see in the smoke, but Les told me that maybe the girls had smelled the smoke and ran downstairs. So we both ran for the stairs and when we got to the bottom we could see the front door was open. I raced outside and there were our three girls shivering on the front porch in their night clothes."

While her husband ran to a neighbor's to phone the fire department, Emily held her children close and cried. After a moment she thought to congratulate her girls on having the sense to run from the house when they smelled smoke. "No, Mommy," came the reply from Rachel, "I did not smell the smoke at first. Someone came in and woke me up and told me to go downstairs. Then she went away." The older two girls, though shaken and still groggy from sleep, reported that they too remembered being awakened by someone who told them to leave their rooms.

"Kimberly and Kate did not remember things too clearly," says Emily, "but I knew who to thank. I took a deep breath and said a silent thank you to the ghost. She may have saved our lives."

In a few minutes the fire department arrived and managed to extinguish a smoldering blaze in the attic caused by careless workmanship on the part of the electricians hired to rewire the home. Before leaving the home, however, the firemen commented to Mr. Kertes that it was fortunate that the fire was discovered early, since, if left undetected, it could well have erupted into a major blaze. Once again, Emily knew who to thank.

Eventually the home was repaired and life returned to normal there. Throughout the subsequent years, however, the enigmatic spirit continued to express herself in subtle ways. "After the girls grew up and moved out," Emily says with a smile, "I would hear footsteps at night walking down the hall to their rooms and I thought that the ghost was wondering where her babies were."

"In 1978, we sold the house and the day we moved, I was the last one to leave. I remember that I stood in the kitchen and closed my eyes and said another thank you to the spirit. Then I told her she was welcome to move with Les and me to our new home. To tell you the truth, by then I sort of felt like she was a close friend. However, I think she stayed. I never saw or heard anything in our new house. I kind of missed her."

If she is still there today, the current residents might count themselves lucky to have a spectral nanny on call twenty-four hours a day. She is not the fearful sort of phantom encountered by Marie Dudeck in her home on Boots Street, but a gentle, kind spirit, intent only on helping and protecting the people living in "her" house.

2
The Ghost of the Missing Aviator
Purdue University
West Lafayette, Indiana

Courage is the price that Life exacts for granting peace.
The soul that knows it not, knows no realease.

Amelia Earhart[1]

She was young and fearless and her daring escapades caught the attention of a nation. With her life she pushed the limits of what it was assumed a woman could do and became the symbol of the American spirit. With her mysterious death, she left a legend and mystery that endure to this day. Moreover, if the strange tales told around airplane hangar number one at Purdue University are to be believed, perhaps she left more...an enigmatic phantom that is said to linger in the area where she lived some of her last and happiest days.

Most Americans are familiar with the story of Amelia Earhart. Her name and fame have become indelibly chiseled into the history of America and particularly the history of aviation. Since her sudden disappearance in 1937, her legend has grown and her fate is still hotly debated by some. What many in Indiana are unaware of, however, is their state's role in the life and death of the aviator. In fact, one of the premier educational institutions of our state played a key role in the life of Amelia Earhart and an inadvertent role in her mysterious disappearance.

It has been said that long before the name of Amelia Earhart became known across our nation and world, she was a woman destined for greatness. Born on July 24, 1897, in Atchison, Kansas, Amelia began life in a family of moderate means. Her father, an attorney, apparently suffered from a lifelong struggle with alcoholism. In addition to the effects of his drinking problem on his family, this disease caused Alfred Earhart to go through a series of jobs, often leaving the family in dire economic circumstances.

Much of her early years were spent in Kansas City, where her family lived in a home given to them by her maternal grandfather. Despite the family difficulties, Earhart's early childhood seems to have been a tranquil one. Considered a tomboy in her day, Earhart and her young sister, Murial (known as "Pidge"), spent much of their childhood running free in the woods and bluffs that surrounded their home, the traditional skirts and pinafores of the day replaced with makeshift gym suits sewn by their mother. Together they would wander away the summer days, looking for adventure and excitement.

As Earhart would later write:

> Whether it was considered the thing to do or not was irrelevant. As a little girl I had ridden my buggy in the stable; I had once climbed up on a delivery horse; I had explored the fearsome caves in the cliffs overlooking the Missouri; I had invented a trap and caught a chicken.... and I knew there was more fun and excitement in life that I would have time to enjoy."[2]

As Amelia progressed through school, she showed herself to be a bright and inquisitive student. She excelled in the limited athletics allowed girls of her time, but her chief loves were books and animals. Often during family trips to visit her grandparents' stately home in Atchison, Amelia would spend hours on end in her grandfather's library, poring over books on travel and world history. As she would later remark, from these books she would cull a taste for the adventure she would pursue later in life.

About the time that Amelia entered young adulthood, however, life began to change for her. Due to her father's alcoholism, the family was forced to move several times as he continued to change jobs. Often they were left near abject poverty, and the Earhart sisters were forced to make do with secondhand clothes.

Still, in 1916, Amelia's mother was able to scrape together sufficient funds to enroll her in the Ogontz School in Rydal, Pennsylvania. At this upper-class girls' preparatory school, Earhart thrived both intellectually and socially. While her inquisitive nature and strong opinions on controversial issues often put her at odds with her fellow classmates, in general she was well liked by both staff and students. Significantly, it was while at Ogontz that Amelia began to be a strong proponent of women's rights, including the right to vote and choose a career. While such views were considered radical at the time, Amelia devoted herself to the cause of women's suffrage and helped organize at least one presentation on the subject for the school.

Earhart's life took another turn in December 1917. Visiting her sister, who was serving as a Red Cross nurse in Toronto, Amelia was touched by the plight of wounded soldiers returning from World War I. Abruptly, Earhart dismissed her plans of returning to school and signed up for a concentrated course in nursing from the Red Cross. Soon she found a job as a nurse's aide in a nearby military hospital, where her innate compassion and empathy made her a natural healer. So taken was she with her experience that for a time she resolved to become a doctor. However, fate would soon take a hand and change the course of her life forever.

In 1918, a friend invited Amelia to a barnstorming exhibition at a county fair near Toronto. As she watched the stunt fliers complete their loops and rolls, she became flushed with excitement. When one of the fliers unexpectedly swooped low over the crowd, Amelia calmly stood still as the crowd around dove for cover. Eyes fixed on the bi-winged

Photo: Purdue University

Amelia Earhart standing on the tarmac next to her plane at the Purdue University airfield.

aircraft as it flew past, Earhart knew she was catching a glimpse of her future.

Returning to her work at the military hospital, Amelia began to search out former pilots among her patients. Often she would sit enthralled for hours, listening to tales of their daring aeronautic exploits. As she did so, she felt a keen desire rise within her to experience the freedom and excitement of flight.

It would not be until January 1921 that Earhart would first get to experience that thrill. By then, Amelia was living in Los Angeles with her parents once again and working at a local telephone company. Seeking a distraction from a recently broken engagement, Earhart signed up for flight classes at a nearby airfield, much to the chagrin of the flight instructors.

It should be noted that, while there were other women fliers in the air at the time, the concept of a female pilot was still considered unique. However, Earhart quickly won over her skeptical instructors by showing a keen intellect, an insatiable curiosity about all aspects of flight, and a natural instinct for flying. Earhart, it was said by one instructor, was born to soar.

By the next summer, Amelia was the proud owner of her very first aircraft–a new Kinner Airster. Less than a year after she took possession of the craft, she piloted the little plane to 14,000 feet, much higher than any woman had flown previously. Already this daring aviator was redefining what airplanes, and particularly women pilots, could do.

However, in 1924 Amelia's spirits plunged once more. With the divorce of her parents, she sold her beloved Airster in order to move with her mother and sister to Medford, Massachusetts. There she took a job as a social worker at a settlement house for immigrants, teaching English to children. Her natural enthusiasm and caring nature earned her the respect and affection of parents and students alike. Still, however, deep within her Amelia felt the call of the sky.

Joining the American Aeronautical Society in Boston, Earhart found opportunities to continue to fly. As her younger sister later recalled:

> Amelia became known to most of the freelance pilots around Boston as a woman who could not only fly well, but also knew about engine performance, tensile strengths and something about instrument flying. Mechanics at the field soon found out she was not adverse to getting

her hands greasy. She watched, asked questions and helped service her plane. Pilots and mechanics liked and respected Amelia."[3]

Amelia's fame as an aeronautical engineer began to take shape in 1929, when she was invited to become the first woman to fly across the Atlantic Ocean. Although only a passenger on the trip, the national and world press embraced her daring spirit and sparkling personality. Suddenly Earhart was drawing crowds wherever she went. Sagely, Amelia used her new-found fame to generate interest and necessary funds for her future projects. Quitting her job, she decided to devote herself completely to becoming a world-class pilot.

In 1929 Earhart competed in the first Women's Air Derby from Santa Monica California, to Cleveland, Ohio. The next year she set a women's air speed record of 181.8 miles per hour over a three-kilometer course. In 1931 she set an altitude record of 18,541 feet in a Autogyro—a craft that was the predecessor of modern helicopters. She also was instrumental in establishing the first airline service to shuttle passengers between New York, Washington and Philadelphia. Meanwhile she also served as President of "The Ninety Nines," the first women's aeronautical association, as well as working as aviation editor for *Cosmopolitan* magazine. In the American consciousness, a star was being born.

On February 7, 1931, Amelia Earhart married George P. Putnam, whom she had met while planning her trip across the Atlantic. In later years, Putnam would serve as both publicity agent and manager for Earhart's career. It was a career that, like the woman herself, would soon reach unprecedented heights.

On May 20 of the next year, Amelia climbed into the cockpit for her most daring venture yet. She was determined to fly across the Atlantic Ocean once again, this time as pilot and this time alone. It was exactly five years since Charles Lindbergh had begun his first solo trek across the expanse and since his flight, fourteen others had died trying to duplicate his feat.

Nevertheless, as the dauntless Earhart climbed into her plane, her spirits were high. Nearly fifteen hours later, after countless difficulties and at least one near crash into the ocean, she landed in Londonderry, Northern Ireland. Now her international acclaim rose still higher. She was awarded France's Cross of the Legion of Honor, as well as the National

Geographic Society's Gold Medal. Everywhere she went she was lauded with honor and acclaim.

The next few years brought yet more distinction for the young woman. She continued to set new aeronautical records, as well as becoming a well-known lecturer and celebrity. She was also a vocal proponent of women's rights and served as a role model for a generation of young women across the globe.

Then in the fall of 1935, Amelia Earhart came to Indiana, to Purdue University. The impetus for her association with the school had come a year earlier, when Earhart had been the featured speaker at a "Women Changing the World" conference held in New York City by the *New York Herald Tribune*. In introducing her talk, Earhart remarked that while she had been asked to address her talk to youth, she did so with trepidation because, "the ancients, such as I am, should be listening to young ideas rather than pointing up opportunities in a world which has the elders decidedly on the run!"

While Miss Earhart went on to hold the rapt attention of her audience for the next hour, there was one man present who listened to her remarks with particular interest. He was Dr. Edward C. Elliott, president of Purdue University. Renowned as a visionary leader and progressive educator, it was well known that Elliott had long held a special interest in aviation, as well as a strong commitment to higher education for women. Indeed, thanks to Elliott's vision and ceaseless efforts, Purdue had become the first college in the United States to boast of a fully functional airport equipped for both day or night flight, and it had the largest and best aeronautical engineering department of any school in the nation.

However, by encouraging higher education for women, Elliott was faced with a more serious challenge. Though Purdue had a higher percentage of women enrolled than most public institutions of the time, the president had publicly lamented the fact that of the over six thousand students enrolled, only one thousand were female, and female instructors were still a rarity. Clearly, Elliott was searching for a way of encouraging the enrollment of women at Purdue, and to encourage those enrolled to stretch their understanding of a woman's role in American society.

In Amelia Earhart, Elliott saw a way of advancing both of these interests. The addition of Earhart to the Purdue staff would be a coup for the president and add to the already prestigious reputation of his school.

After Earhart was done speaking, President Elliott wasted no time in making arrangements to meet her and her husband for dinner that night at the Coffee House Club in Manhattan. After dinner, Elliott came directly to the point. "We want you at Purdue," Elliott told Amelia bluntly. Unflappable, Earhart replied casually, "I'd like that if it could be arranged. What would you think I should do?"

Thus was the beginning of Earhart's association with Purdue. By the time Elliott parted company with his new-found friends that evening, the pair had conceived of the basis for their arrangement. Oh June 25, President Elliott announced that Earhart had accepted a position with Purdue. In making his announcement, he noted

> Miss Earhart represents better than any other young woman of this generation the spirit and the courageous skill of what may be called the new pioneering. The University believes that Amelia Earhart will help us to see and attack successfully many unsolved problems.

So it was that in November 1935 Amelia Earhart came to Purdue to assume the role of an visiting faculty member in the Women's Careers Department, as well as a advisor to the Aeronautics Department. As such, Earhart was to spend several weeks each semester on campus, living in a Spartan room at South Hall, a women's residence hall. While there, Earhart would occasionally give special lectures or presentations to the student body, but by and large, her duties were simply to interact and influence the students, particularly the young women on campus. This, it seems, Amelia did with some relish. As one female student would later recall,

> After dinner...as many students who could would follow Miss Earhart into my room and sit around on the floor (she sat on the floor too) and talk and listen. She was adaptable, easy and informal. It was during those times especially that we got to know some of the underlying beliefs and hopes and dreams that motivated our distinguished guest. She believed in women's intelligence, their ability to learn and their ability to do whatever they wanted to. There was no question that she, through her own achievements and persuasiveness, was an effective catalyst to heretofore unthinkable thoughts for all of us. [4]

It should be noted that not all at the school were so generous with their praise. One dean scoffed that Earhart was "not academically qualified" to be a member of the university faculty. Others at the university were horrified by Earhart's dress and casual manners, which tended to fly in the face of conventional Midwestern standards for women of the time. At least one professor's wife complained to President Elliott concerning Earhart's "scandalous behavior in being seen in public, (and particularly a local soda fountain), wearing *men's pants!*" President Elliott, to his credit, seems to have ignored the protest and generally it can be said that Earhart enjoyed the support and admiration of the campus community.

Meanwhile, Amelia used her time while not at Purdue to maintain a rigorous schedule of speaking engagements and public appearances, as well as continuing flying whenever possible. It was a happy, fulfilling time for her. As her husband, George Putnam, would later write, "[I think] she found her time at Purdue as one of the most satisfying adventures of her life." It was also a time in which Earhart began to reassess her career and plan her next project in aviation. When that plan emerged, it would prove to be an incredibly ambitious and ultimately fatal one.

It was announced that Amelia Earhart would attempt to fly around the world. While this feat alone would not be a first (the circumnavigation of the world by airplane having been accomplished at least twice by 1937), two aspects of the flight would make Earhart's project unique: first, it would be accomplished for the first time by a woman and second, unlike the other around the world flights, Earhart's course would take her roughly along the equator, along the longest route possible. It would be one of the most daring undertakings in the history of aeronautics and it was to be the last of Amelia's long distance flights. As she remarked to the press,

> I have a feeling that there is just about one more good flight left in me and I hope this trip is it. Anyway, when I have finished this job, I mean to give up long distance "stunt" flying.[5]

At first, the dream of an around the world flight seemed beyond the grasp of even the great Amelia Earhart. One of the most challenging obstacles in her way would be financial; the Lockheed Electra that Amelia had decided was necessary for such a flight would cost well in excess of a hundred thousand dollars, well beyond her means. Without major financial backing, her dream would never leave the ground.

However, once again Purdue University and President Edward Elliott came into the picture. At a dinner party at the home of President Elliott one evening, Amelia was called upon to talk about her views on the future of aviation and in particular the plans for her next flight. After candidly noting the financial difficulties she faced in mounting such a project, even the unflappable Earhart was shocked when Elliott casually suggested that Purdue supply her with a "flying laboratory" in which to make her flight.

As ambitious as the suggestion might seem, at least one dinner guest, Purdue alumnus and benefactor David Ross, immediately offered to donate $50,000 for the purpose. In the next few weeks, another $30,000 was received as gifts from several other companies and individuals and "The Amelia Earhart Fund for Aeronautical Research" was begun.

In short order, the project bore fruit and in June 1936 Amelia Earhart took delivery of her new "flying laboratory." In receiving her gift, Earhart publicly professed her "profound gratitude and appreciation to Purdue University, its students and staff." So grateful were Earhart and her husband that at first he suggested the plane be painted in the "old gold and black," the colors of Purdue, but this idea was vetoed by aviation officials because such colors might make the airplane less visible from the ground.

Shortly after Earhart took possession of her prized new aircraft, she began an intense process of testing and evaluating it in preparation for her round the world quest. The Purdue University airport became one of Amelia's testing grounds and hangar number one, where the craft was normally stored, became one of her chief haunts. Stories suggest that Earhart began to spend long hours at the hangar, examining every inch of her airplane in preparation for the flight before her.

The flight plan was a strenuous one. Aided by navigator Fred Noonan, Earhart was to fly from Oakland, California, to Honolulu, then south to the equator and, by legs of various lengths, to fly west around the girth of the earth, eventually arriving back in Oakland.

Even from the start the journey seemed doomed. The flight from Oakland to Hawaii was uneventful but on takeoff from Honolulu for the second leg of their epic journey, Earhart and Noonan crashed the Electra, sustaining serious damage to the aircraft. Badly disappointed, Earhart and Noonan accompanied their plane back to California to the Lockheed factory, where workmen volunteered to work around the clock to repair the damage.

Eventually, after a delay of several months, Earhart took off again in early June, this time heading east from Oakland toward Miami and then on to San Juan, Puerto Rico. From there, the pair made their way across the Atlantic, landing in Dakar on the coast of Africa before flying on across the Arabian Peninsula to India, landing in Calcutta.

From India, Earhart piloted her aircraft through southwest Asia, landing in Papua, New Guinea on June 29. By now the pair had been in the air for nearly three weeks and had completed twenty-two thousand miles. Only seven thousand miles lay before Amelia Earhart and home. If all went well, they would arrive in California on the Fourth of July. However, the pair knew that between them and the American coast lay the longest and most dangerous leg of their journey.

At the precisely 10:00 A.M. on July 2, 1937, Amelia Earhart and Fred Noonan took off from New Guinea for Howland Island, a tiny atoll that would serve as a way station on their journey homeward. They would never be seen again...alive.

Throughout the night, officials in both New Guinea and in Howland waited for word of the pair's progress. Finally, some nineteen hours later, the *USS Itasca,* anchored off Howland, which had been receiving radio reports from Earhart throughout the flight, received a disturbing report via radio.

"We must be on you but cannot see you. Gas is running low–only one-half hour left. Been unable to reach you by radio. We are flying at one thousand feet." The ship radioed back a message asking for the plane's precise location, but received no reply.

Eighteen minutes later another message was received from Earhart, this time asking help from the ship in determining their position. Again, when the ship tried to reply, no response was received. At 8:14 P.M. came a final desperate communication from Earhart and then the radio fell utterly and finally silent. Amelia Earhart had disappeared forever.

In the ensuing days and weeks, one of the most massive and thorough searches in the history of aviation was mounted. The U.S. Navy lent ships and airplanes for the search and help was elicited from other governments to aid in the hunt. Yet all was in vain. In time over one thousand square miles of sea were searched from air and ship, yet from that day to this one, no trace of the famed aviator has been found.

With the passing decades, innumerable theories have been advanced to explain the sudden and some might say mysterious disappearance of Earhart and Noonan. Theories ranging from government intrigue to UFO abduction have been forwarded but none have been found convincing. In the end, the fate of Amelia Earhart remains as mysterious today as it was in 1937.

The tragic disappearance of Amelia Earhart plunged a nation into grief ,and the fruitless search that followed left more questions in its wake, including questions that still puzzle historians today. However, while nothing has been heard from the daring aviator since the day of her last radio transmission, her story has lived on. The years following have seen the story of Amelia Earhart make its way into countless books, movies and documentary television programs. Her face has been found gracing everything from postage stamps to T-shirts and the Amelia Earhart Society has been established to promote her memory and further the causes she began.

By now the life and death of this young woman have passed squarely into the realm of American legend and on into the fuzzy netherworld of folklore. It should not be surprising, then, that legends regarding the missing aviator have sprung up in at least one place where she spent her last and perhaps happiest, days: Purdue University.

Purdue has long been proud of its association with Amelia Earhart. Mementos of her life and especially her time at the school have been carefully preserved at the Purdue University Archives, and stories of her time at the school have been endlessly recounted.

However, somewhere amid the official documents and historical artifacts preserved at Purdue, one finds an underlying essence of folklore concerning the aviator: strange, mysterious legends, for which there are no official university records. Legends that hint that perhaps Amelia Earhart might have left more than her aviation legacy to the school. Listening to the tales, one might be tempted to wonder if perhaps a part of the famous aviator lingers still at Purdue.

It should be carefully noted that the university itself puts little stock in the tales of the spectral presence of Amelia Earhart at the school. As one university official put it, "we are a no-ghost zone here at Purdue." Indeed, the official university archives contains no hint of any spectral tales centered around the university. Others at the school, while acknowledging that the legends exist, tend to explain them away as the product of urban legend, and perhaps this is the case. However, it must be said that for many years tales of ghostly activity have been told around campus–tales that are linked, in the collective mind of generations of college students, to the doomed aviator.

Sally Jonas* is one of those who can tell such tales, having heard them as a child from her father.

"The stories were really part of our family tradition. Dad came from Ireland and he loved to tell stories–all kinds of stories. But the ghost of the airplane hangar was one of his favorites," the thirty-five year old nurse now says, a wisp of fond nostalgia creeping into her voice.

"My father came to America in the late thirties or early forties. He came to Indiana because his brother, my uncle Edwin, was already here. Dad had been a engine mechanic in Dublin, but at first the only job he could get here was working as a janitor at the Purdue airfield. He would work all night cleaning things up and then when he was finished, he used to help some of the mechanics work on the planes. That was how he got to know the guys at the hangar shop, and eventually he was hired on as a mechanic."

Sally goes on to relate that her father often told her and her sister that when he began his work as janitor and building maintenance worker at the airfield, he was unaware of any ghostly tales associated with the structure.

"According to what he told us, for the first six months he was working there, he did not even know that Amelia Earhart had ever been to Purdue, much less that she had worked on the plane in which she would die at that hangar."

This was to suddenly change, however, late one night when Sally's father was taking his dinner break in the hangar with several of the airplane mechanics. To hear Sally tell the tale:

> Dad and two or three of his cronies were standing apart from the airplanes a little distance, sipping coffee. It was a bitterly cold night in January and they were as far from the main hangar doors as they could get, trying to stay warm. Dad told us kids that as they stood there talking, suddenly one of the young mechanics came tearing around the corner going like eighty. Dad said that he was white as a sheet and running so hard he was not looking where he was going and he tripped over one of the guys standing there and went sprawling across the floor.

Sally goes on to relate that after picking the young man up and trying to calm him down, her father and the other mechanics asked the young man the cause of his alarm. "There was someone back there in the tool room," the young man exclaimed, pointing to the far end of the hangar. "Someone who wasn't real."

The young man told the group that he had gone into the aircraft tool shop to find a wrench for a maintenance job he was finishing up. As he bent over the large workbench, looking for the needed tool, he suddenly became aware of the feeling that he was being watched. Repeatedly, he looked up from his search, only to find himself alone in the room, yet he could not escape the feeling that he was being scrutinized. Finally finding the wrench he need for his job, he stood up and was about to beat a hasty path from room when he saw, standing the corner of the room, a figure.

"Dad said the mechanic told him that it was just a shape–like a person in silhouette, but three dimensional. This young guy was so startled he threw the wrench he had just picked up at the figure but the wrench went right through it and the figure suddenly disappeared."

As strange as this story sounded to Sally's father, stranger still was the reaction of the other mechanics. "Dad told us kids that when he heard the story this young man was telling, he was inclined to either laugh or smell his breath for booze," Sally recalls with a smile. "But the other mechanics just looked at the kid for a minute and then one of the told him real directly, 'It's OK. She won't hurt you. Just shut up and don't tell anybody about it.' Dad said when he heard the word 'she' he knew that something was up but he did not want to ask too many questions. So he kind of quietly shut his lunch box and they all went back to work. Later he talked to a supervisor," Sally continues, "and he kind of quietly told him about Amelia Earhart being at Purdue before her last flight. That was the first Dad knew of it."

However, this would not be the last that Sally's father would hear about he strange figure said to haunt hangar number one. According to Sally, the second time her father ran across someone who claimed an encounter with the ghost of the area was almost a year later.

"Dad told my sister Jane and me that the second time was just before Christmas. He remembered the time of year because he and the other mechanics had just finished decorating the outside of the hangar with a few lights and there was a tree set up in the break room. According to what Dad told us, he was getting ready to leave the hangar and had come into the break room to grab his lunch box. Sitting there at the table was one of the old time mechanics and as Dad went by, he saw the guy was clutching a cup of coffee with both hands and he was trembling."

Concerned that his co-worker might be ill, Sally said her father paused for a moment to sit down and speak to the man. When asked if he was feeling ill, the mechanic turned and, with a grim look in his eyes, replied that he was thinking of taking early retirement from his job. As a matter of fact, he was thinking of walking out that night and never coming back.

"Dad asked the mechanic–his name was John–why he would do something like that," Sally says, "and John said that he did not want to work in the hangar at night anymore. When Dad asked him why, John told him 'I'm tired of that damn woman pilot coming around and bothering me. I try to ignore her, but she stands there in the corner and watches everything that goes on.' Dad told John that he had not seen any pilots in the hangar that night, but that if someone was bothering him, he would help show them to the door."

"At that point, Dad said John put his hand on Dad's shoulder and said 'You don't get it, Pete–this particular pilot is dead.' John then went on to relate the story of Amelia Earhart's association with Purdue and told Sally's father that ever since her disappearance, mechanics working late at night had seen a figure matching the description of Earhart standing in the shadows of hangar number one."

According to Sally Jonas, at first her father was not inclined to believe the loose talk of the spirit. "You have to remember that my dad was a hardscrabble Irishman who grew up on the streets of Dublin. He was more inclined to use his fists than he was to believe in something he could not see." Still, with the passing of time Pete had to admit that more and more people reported seeing or experiencing the presence of a phantom in the precincts of hangar number one.

Sally's sister Jane remembers one of the more unusual stories as it was reported to her by her father. "Dad was not there when this one happened," she recalls with a smile, "but he sure heard about it. It happened during World War II, when the government was doing some sort of research on experimental aircraft fuel. Anyway, they came into Purdue and took over one of the hangars for about six weeks. Oonly those people with secret clearance could keep working on the planes at the airfield. They ran barbed wire and posted armed guards and the whole bit.

"My father said that because he was still not yet a naturalized citizen (that did not happened till the early 50s), he could not get clearance to work in the hangar so rather than let him go, his boss had him temporarily transferred to another part of the university. About six weeks later, when the army had moved out, he was allowed to go back to work at the hangar."

After Pete had returned to his work at airport, he heard yet another story of the appearance of the phantom of the airfield. "Years later Dad told me that when he got back to working at the airfield, some of the mechanics were laughing one night about something that had happened when the army was there. Dad asked them what had happened and one of the guys said, 'Old Amelia decided to scare the hell out of one of the solider boys they had out here.' "

The worker then went on to relate that he was revamping an airplane engine late one night during the army's presence when he was startled to hear the sound of several shots being fired from a rifle just a few yards away. A veteran of the First World War, the mechanic instinctively dove for cover, but after a moment of silence, he and several others braved their way outside to check on the source of the commotion.

"This mechanic told my dad that there was a army sentry out there clutching his rifle in one arm and screaming something into a radio. He was white as a sheet and obviously emotionally distraught. He kept on screaming something about an intruder into the radio and ordering the mechanics back into the building but they just stood there staring at the man. They had the attitude that this was the most interesting thing that had happened there in months and they were not going to miss out on the fun."

Eventually, a number of soldiers, including the sentry's superior officer appeared from the darkness of the field and began to sweep the area with bright lights. As the airplane mechanics (who had still refused to retreat to the hangar despite numerous orders to do so) listened, the young sentry was debriefed by his senior officer. Still half hysterical, the sentry said that he was walking his patrol that dark night when he saw, approaching him, the figure of someone in pilot's gear.

The sentry called out a challenge and ordered to figure to stop, but it continued past him, going in the direction of hangar number one. Undaunted, the sentry called out the order to halt and that the area was restricted. When this challenge was similarly ignored, the sentry fired several warning shots into the air, but still the figure continued on. Finally shouting a warning that this was the last opportunity to stop, the solider shouldered his weapon and took aim at the figure, aiming to wound the intruder. However, before he could shoot the figure disappeared, seeming to evaporate into the dark night air.

"The mechanic who told Dad this story said that he heard this sentry, who was almost in tears, swear to his commanding officer that he had ordered the figure to stop but instead of stopping the figure just moved toward hangar number one. Then just before it got there, it just sort of was gone.

"According to what Dad heard, the officer was a bit dubious about the story. He thought that maybe someone had been messing around and playing tricks on the sentry, but he had the area searched anyway and no one was found. Then he looked over and saw this group of mechanics who had been standing there watching this whole thing. This colonel came over and asked the mechanics if they knew anything about what had happened, or if they had seen anything strange that night. The mechanic who talked to Dad said he just looked at this army colonel and said 'We ain't seen nothing sir, we are just maintenance guys but we do know this: Your boy over then has been messed with by a ghost and she probably doesn't appreciate being shot at.' "

The reaction of the officer is perhaps best left to the imagination.

Exactly when the stories of a specter haunting hangar number one became associated with Amelia Earhart cannot precisely be determined. It is thought that since the first reports of its presence came in the early 1940s, just a few years after the mysterious disappearance of Earhart, it was only natural that the stories would become linked to her. Others have pointed out that several descriptions of the enigmatic figure, though vague, did fit the description of a slight woman wearing a pilot's uniform.

While some might argue the validity of such stories, the perspective of one Purdue University official must also be considered: "Anytime you have a famous figure attached to an institution who dies tragically and even mysteriously, it is only natural that any strange events there will be attributed to that person's ghost."

Details, particularly historical verification, of these legends are tenuous at best. No record exists at Purdue regarding the army having ever spent time there during World War II, and one airfield worker interviewed noted that while he had been at the Purdue Airport thirty years, he had never heard such stories nor seen anything inexplicable.

Yet the stories persist. According to a newspaper article from the late 1970s, one student working in a newly renovated office in hangar number one was startled, late one afternoon as she was leaving the office, to hear the deafening roar of an antique aircraft being started in her immediate vicinity. "It sounded like it was right there in the office with me!" the girl later told the reporter. However, after she fled from the office, the sound abruptly was silenced. A check revealed that no aircraft had been started in the hangar that afternoon.

Interestingly, according to university legend, the apparition has been encountered not only within the confines of the Purdue Airport, but in the residence hall where Earhart lived while on campus as well.

Marvis Boscher, who was manager at the hall for many years, says that girls living there told stories of cold drafts being felt in the end room on the first floor (where Earhart had once resided) and of windows opening of their own volition. While Ms. Bosher attributes these stories to the folklore often generated on college campuses, students living there seem to put some stock in the tales. Former students tell of occasionally glimpsing a shadowy figure of a short woman with close-cropped hair lurking in the hallway outside the room. Uniformly, the tales relate that when approached the figure seems to dissolve into thin air. Other stories tell of hearing the sound of an old-fashioned typewriter clicking from the vacant room late at night when Earhart was known to do her writing.

Perhaps, as some suggest, the tales associated with the ghost of Amelia Earhart at Purdue University are nothing more than the result of college folklore and the collective imagination of the campus. If this is the case, then surely this does little to diminish their mystery and charm. The stories are a part of the legacy of this remarkable young woman, who, with flair and daring style, created a unique place for herself in the tapestry of American legend.

3

A Trio of School Spirits
Indianapolis, Indiana

When most of us look back at our years in elementary and high school, our minds are filled with fond memories of football games, school dances and a seemingly endless stream of book reports. Commonly, we associate schools with the lively bustle of students and teachers and the innocence of youth. Visit any school as classes are ending for the day and one cannot help but be overwhelmed with the rush of frantic noise and activity and the incredible sense of the vitality of youth.

However, visit these places of education after dark and a somewhat more somber atmosphere can be found. Empty halls echo back the sound of footsteps and vacant classrooms seem steeped in a deathly silence. In moments such as these, it is not hard to imagine that such places of life might also harbor something else. Perhaps the spirits of those who have long since departed the building, and even life, might linger there still.

Just ask Mike Richardson.*

Mike Richardson is not the sort of person one might expect to talk about ghost stories, much less find himself caught up in one. The pragmatic Richardson readily describes himself as a "burly, knuckle dragging, no nonsense cop." It is true that to first meet this thirty-year veteran of a metropolitan Indianapolis police force, one cannot help but be struck with the impression of a thoroughly hard-nosed, streetwise officer. With his intimidating 6'3" frame, thick black hair, and bushy mustache, Officer Richardson is a man who commands immediate respect.

However, despite his outward appearance, to speak to Officer Richardson is to quickly discover a thoughtful, gentle man who genuinely cares about his profession and those he has sworn to protect. Even when he speaks of the rigors of life as a street cop, his eyes shine with a warmth and kindness belying his gruff exterior.

Still, as with most policemen, a streak of pragmatism runs deep in Officer Richardson, making it difficult for him to acknowledge the strange and somewhat inexplicable circumstances into which his job has occasionally thrust him. "On my best days, I am just a decent street cop," he says with a smile. "I don't know about this ghost stuff. I just know that there is something there."

The "there" Officer Richardson is describing is actually three school buildings in Indianapolis, where strange occurrences have been reported for many years. Like many in his profession, Mike has been in a unique position to encounter these strange occurrences, since his patrol duties have brought him into many diverse areas of Indianapolis, many times late at night.

Mike Richardson is not as unique in this respect as one might think. In fact, despite their professional, matter-of-fact demeanor, a great many police officers can tell odd tales of inexplicable things they have experienced during the course of their duties. By the very nature of their vocation, police often work late at night in empty buildings (where spirits are want to manifest themselves) and often work in death and near-death situations. As many police officers can attest, settings such as these sometimes give rise to odd and even strange happenings.

In the case of Mike Richardson, through his decades of serving his community, his duties have also drawn him into this strange dimension of police work, a dimension not covered by training manuals and police guidelines. On several occasions over the past several years, Officer Richardson has found himself confronted with several baffling circumstances that have taken him from the pragmatic life of a "street cop" and, some might suggest, thrust him squarely into the realm of Indiana ghostlore.

In the annals of America ghostlore, haunted schools from the elementary to the university level are commonplace. Stories from across our nation tell of unquiet spirits said to walk the halls of many of our educational institutions. Interestingly, Officer Richardson has encountered not one but three such cases in recent years.

The first of these is a small building now used to house the administrative offices for a school district on the outskirts of Indianapolis. Made of indigenous stone, now covered with ivy, this historic structure was built in 1870 to serve as a local Quaker Meeting House. A nearby Quaker cemetery gives tribute to the generations of Quaker settlers who worshipped at the structure and passed to their eternal reward. If the tales told of the place are true, however, perhaps a few of these solid Quakers might not have passed away as completely as some might wish.

In 1965, the Quaker congregation moved to another more modern building and the old stone church was given over for use by the local school corporation. The internal structure was then renovated to accommodate offices throughout the building and, significantly, in the mid 1970s, an intricate alarm system was installed. This alarm system would later give credence to some long-held rumors regarding the building.

Almost from the moment the school system assumed control of the structure, stories began to circulate that something strange was occurring within its walls. One maintenance staff person who worked late at the site during its renovation reported the sound of footsteps echoing through the building. Several times the workman rose from his labors to tour the building, but each time he found it empty, with all the doors locked from the inside.

At one point, he later recalled, he plainly heard the sound of someone slowly walking through the main hallway of the building. Sure that he would now catch whatever intruder had been pestering him, he ran to the door of the room where he was working and jumped into the hallway. As he did so, he quickly hit the light switch next to him on the wall, illuminating the hallway in bright light. The hallway was utterly vacant yet as he listened intently, he could hear the sound of footsteps progressing down the hallway, going up to and then through a solid partition that blocked the far end of the hall. Understandably, he cut short his work that night and went home early rather than continue to share the building with an unseen presence.

Eventually, the school system elected to install a set of alarms in the small building to provide security during the nighttime hours. These alarms' sensors were set into two patterns: first, contact alarms were installed on all windows and doors, forming a perimeter that would first have to be penetrated. Then motion detectors were put in place throughout the building to detect the movement of an intruder. By watching the sequence of alarms, monitored through a computer, security workers could actually trace the progress of an intruder through the building and alert the authorities.

However, according to Officer Richardson, this system has often exhibited strange operational problems. "We have had a number of alarms down there that were really curious," Officer Richardson recalls. "We continue to have scenarios where the alarm company will call us and say that they have motion alarms in zone two or three of the building but no perimeter alarms have been set off. You would have to penetrate the perimeter alarms to get in the place, but no perimeter alarms have been set off. This has happened at least once a month in the last several years."

While some maintenance crews in the building have suggested that the motion detected by the alarm sensors was caused by drafts in the building, what makes this phenomena doubly curious is that, by monitoring the motion alarms as they go off, alarms company workers have been able to trace the progress of whatever is moving from one zone to another. Further, since most motion sensors are geared to detect the movement of large bodies, the idea that such alarms could be triggered by rodents can be similarly discounted. "It sure is curious." Mike Richards remarks.

Curious indeed.

However mysterious the goings-on at the Old Quaker Meeting House as it is known, they are by no means the only puzzling phenomena occurring in school facilities in and around Indianapolis. Indeed, in central Indianapolis, there stands an elementary school that has been the scene of even more eerie occurrences.

According to Officer Richardson, for many years the school was the dominion of a much-beloved principal. Well liked by both students and staff members, this benevolent administrator was staunchly devoted to the school and students in his charge. One night several years ago, the principal came to work just as the janitorial staff was finishing the daily cleaning of the school. Noting that he had paperwork to do in his office, he told the maintenance staff to go home for the rest of the evening and he would lock up the school when he left in a few hours. Unfortunately, the principal never left the school that night. In fact, some say that he has never left at all.

The next morning, staff arriving early for the school day found their beloved principal in his office, dead of an apparent heart attack. Though grief swept through the school and community, it was said at the time that he had died as he might have wished–looking over the welfare of the school he loved so well.

If this sentiment is true, then perhaps it might help explain some of the uncanny events that are said to have taken place in the school since that night. These are events that stretch the imagination and suggest to some that this much-admired administrator is still concerned with the state of the school to which he had devoted his life.

While working late at night, several of the maintenance staff have reported objects moving seemingly of their own volition. One male staff person reported watching as a bottle of cleaning fluid dislodged itself from a shelf in a storage closet and arced through the air, settling gently about six feet away. Another member of the janitorial staff, whom Officer Richardson describes as a "pleasant, sturdy Indiana farm type gal" reported to him that mop buckets filled with water have been known to occasionally disappear from where they have been left, only to be later found in another wing of the building.

The climax to events at the school came one night when a female janitor, substituting on the midnight shift, called the police dispatcher to report an intruder in the building. "I was on station at another school," Mike recalls, "when I got this call from the dispatcher. I was able to contact the lady by radio and she was panicked. She asked me to come down right away because there was someone in the school with her. I went down there in a hurry, with red lights and siren."

When he arrived, Officer Richardson was confronted with an obviously distraught employee. After taking time to calm her, Officer Richardson asked her the cause of her alarm. She told him that she had been working in the large central hallway of the building when two large doors at the end of the hallway suddenly crashed shut. The doors in question were thick steel fire doors which always remained open except when a fire alarm went off, when they would automatically close to prevent the spread of fire. In this case, however, both doors had simultaneously slammed shut with such explosive force that the steel frame on the door had vibrated.

Convinced that the janitor was telling the truth, Officer Richardson made a thorough inspection of the building but found it totally empty. When he arrived at the central hallway, he found the fire doors shut just as the janitor had described, but as he reopened them he was in for a shock. Much to his surprise, Mike found that each door was attached to the frame by a hydraulic arm, which regulated the speed at which it would close. Even if one tried to slam the door, it would only close at a slow, measured rate. How one such door could slam shut seemed difficult for him to fathom. That two such doors would do so simultaneously seemed utterly impossible. Yet apparently this is exactly what had occurred.

Mike Richardson goes on to relate that after this incident, the janitor in question requested and received a transfer to the day shift at the school. After her startling experience that evening, she refused to ever again work in the building at night.

As strange and mysterious as the phenomena in the administrative building and elementary school might be, however, they pale in comparison with the reports that have been generated from another local high school, where Officer Richardson has been called on several occasions. Like many schools in the Indianapolis area, this particular high school has a regularly assigned police officer to work at the school during the day, and other "street" officers are called into the school at night. For this purpose, school administers have lent a complete set of keys to the local police department, giving the officers access to walk through the school at night checking security. Several times in the last five years, Officer Richardson has been given this responsibility.

Though peaceful and attractive on the outside, this particular high school has been the scene of more than its share of tragedies in past decades. In the 1960s, a student at the school was shot and killed there by a family member who was also a student at the school. Apparently mentally unstable, the sibling was found not guilty of murder by reason of insanity and committed to a mental institution.

Tragic and traumatic though this incident might be, the event that has given rise to the ghostly tales of the school came years later, when a freshman at the school was killed in a traffic accident in the parking lot, immediately in front of the auditorium of the school. The untimely death of the fourteen-year-old girl sent tremors of shock and grief through the school community, as might be imagined. Moreover, in the years since the event, this death has also become attached to some strange and unsettling events that have occurred there.

"I had always heard rumors that there were ghosts in the school," Officer Richardson now recalls, "but I did not pay them any attention. I thought it was just kids telling stories."

Yet not all of the stories attached to the school had their origins in the idle tales of high school students. One of the first people to notice something unusual occurring within the walls of the school was a drama teacher there. Kathy Chamberlin* taught at the school for more than ten years before recently moving to another school district in Indianapolis. Serving both as drama teacher and director of student productions, Ms. Chamberlin was required to spend much of her time in the auditorium, just a few feet from the location where the ill-fated freshman had met her death.

It was here, late at night, that the teacher began to notice some odd and disconcerting disturbances. Ms. Chamberlin told several staff members at the time that she first became aware of the sense of a "presence" in the theater space. "I get the strong feeling that I am not alone there, even when the auditorium is empty," Ms. Chamberlin told a fellow teacher.

As time wore on, this curious feeling was accompanied by other strange incidents. Ms. Chamberlin related that several times, closing up the auditorium late at night after student productions, she caught a fleeting glimpse of a figure moving along the catwalk area high over the stage. At least once, the brave Ms. Chamberlin climbed to the catwalk to search for the person, only to find it empty. However, though the figure had disappeared, at least once it had left rope rigging on the catwalk swaying in its wake.

Interestingly, this seemingly minor report was recently given credence by Troy Taylor, a paranormal researcher who has investigated the school. Taylor, who is president of the American Ghost Society, visited the school to investigate the phenomena said to occur there. In an article in his *Ghosts of the Prairie* magazine, [1] Taylor related that while in the auditorium, one of his investigation team members captured the strange movement of some rigging on the catwalk. According to the article Taylor wrote of the experience,

> Strangely, a video tape filmed (that night) also showed movements of the rope and rigging near the catwalk. We determined that this movement could not have been caused by air currents in the confines of the of the area, as one moment of the tape showed the rigging swaying back and forth and seconds later, the motion had stopped.

Taylor's research also revealed reports from staff members of phantom footsteps heard in the auditorium and the sound of low moans echoing through the dark air of the theater late at night. Further, Taylor's team also noted some strange behavior from one of the seats in the auditorium.

Like most theater style seats, this chair has a spring loaded lower section, which lowers only if weight is placed upon it. Nevertheless, as Taylor's team walked across the stage area, one team member noticed a seat in the first row slowly lower itself, as though some invisible presence had sat down to watch the proceedings.

Going into the house area, the team member raised the seat, only to look back a moment later to find it lowered once again. Now the researcher called the attention of the group to the peculiar movement of the seat and together the team gathered around the seat. Examining the chair, they found it to be in good working order. Though the lower section of the seat was raised several times, it refused to lower itself once again.

Still suspecting that there was something wrong with the mechanics of the chair, Troy Taylor then raised the lower half of the seat and announced to his team that if the seat fell open again, then it must be broken. Ironically, though the seat was observed for the next hour, it remained upright. Subsequent investigation revealed that school staff members had never noted that seat to be broken.

It was also in the auditorium that Mike Richardson first began to suspect the stories he had heard about the school were more than legends. "One time several years ago, I had to walk though the school several nights in a row to cover for another officer," Richardson relates. "I would do a foot walk through the building to make sure that all the lights were out and the doors were locked. The first thing I noticed, curiously, was the strong smell of what seemed to be a woman's cosmetic cream. It was really really strong–almost overpowering."

Officer Richardson goes on to relate that at first the smell was stationary–evidently located in one area of the auditorium. However, on subsequent nights, the curious fragrance began to move, seemingly following him through his tour of the theater.

As odd as this illusive scent seemed, it was not to be Officer Richardson's last encounter with whatever is said to walk the halls of the school. Indeed, his next experience was even more mysterious and unsettling. As Mike tells the story:

> One night, it was a Saturday night, I was parked by the auditorium, just a few feet from where that poor girl had died. I had come in and walked the school, which takes about forty-five minutes if you do it right. Then I came back to the car and tilted one of the seats back to fill out a form and...please do not laugh when I say this but...I could hear breathing in the patrol car. It was clear as a bell, an unmistakable sound and it was right next to me.

Though shocked by the sound emanating from the air around him, Richardson's police instincts immediately took over. He quickly searched the confined area of the car for some natural explanation, yet no explanation presented itself. Further, as he did so, his training in noticing and quickly analyzing details of a situation revealed another unusual aspect of the phenomena.

"You can tell the size of a person by the size of their lungs–the amount of air going in and out," Mike explains. "This was a kid. It was a lighter sound, like less breath was going in and out. It was definitely a child's breath."

It is to Officer Richardson's credit that he did not immediately leave the car at blinding speed. Instead, Mike collected himself, finished writing the report and then drove into the night, leaving the school and whatever presence lingered there behind him in the darkness of the parking lot

However, Officer Richardson would not be able to leave this spirit behind so easily. Several times over the ensuing years, Mike would be called upon to patrol the school area as a part of his regular duties. As a result, on several occasions he has encountered other strange phenomena, both in the school and in the bus garage located a few yards across the parking lot from the site of the young girl's tragic accident.

In order to facilitate the work of both regularly assigned school police officers and the street officers who are frequently called upon to supplement the patrol, the school has provided a small office on the second floor of the bus garage area for their use. Frequently after conducting a walk through on the school, or investigating a traffic report, Officer Richardson would retire to this office to fill out the necessary paperwork or phone in a report to his office. Here Mike has experienced several strange happenings over the past several years.

The first of these occurred in late December 1996. Officer Richardson, as part of his customary nightly patrol, was relegated the duty of walking through the school, after which he drove the short distance to the bus garage to phone in a report to his station house.

Since the night was a brutally cold one, Officer Richardson opened the large bay doors to the garage and pulled his car inside the bus area. In order to prevent fog from forming on the inside windows due to the unequal distribution of heat between the warm garage and his cold car, Officer Richardson decided to leave his car door open when he left the vehicle in the bus bay. In this way, he reasoned, he would be able to leave immediately if called out on an emergency. He then made his way upstairs to the small police office.

He had only been there for a few moments, however, before he was startled to hear the sound of his car door being slammed shut. Quickly retracing his steps downstairs, he found that indeed the car door had closed, yet the bay area was vacant. "I figured someone had come in and shut the door, but I looked around the building and even stepped outside. There wasn't anyone there."

After this disconcerting event, Mike Richardson happened to speak to the regular officer assigned to the school and asked him if he had ever encountered any similar episodes in the bus garage. The officer in question replied that on several occasions, while working in the office late at night, he had been disturbed by the sound of muffled knocking that emanated from the walls of the garage around him. Investigation revealed no logical source for the sounds.

Meanwhile, Officer Richardson has continued to encounter strange events when his duties have brought him to the bus garage office. One of these centered around the same smell of cosmetic cream that had followed him through the auditorium on previous occasions. As Mike now recalls:

One night my wife was with me. Once or twice a month she will come down and ride with me and we went over to the bus garage because I had to fill out an accident report. I remember it was one of the first warm nights in March and I had the doors propped open to let the breeze flow through the area. We were both sitting downstairs in the bus driver's lounge area. They have a large table there and I was sitting there with my wife a few feet away reading a magazine. As I worked on the report, suddenly I was overwhelmed by this smell of a woman's hand cream. It was like it was being stuck right up my nose.

Searching for a rational explanation for the smell, Mike looked around the table and found a scented candle that had been left by a bus driver that day. "I thought, 'This damn thing is about to give me a headache!' " he now recalls. Rising, Mike took the candle, placed it in a nearby women's restroom, returned to his seat at the table, and resumed filling out his forms. Soon, however, Officer Richardson was dismayed to find the smell return.

"It was weird," Mike relates. "There was a good breeze coming through the area but this smell was right up my nose." Looking around, Mike noticed his wife's purse lying a few feet from him on the table. Somewhat testily, he rose again, asking his wife "What the hell do you have in this thing?" He then very deliberately picked up the purse and placed it several feet downwind from the table.

By now feeling a bit wearied by the distractions of the night, Officer Richardson once more sat down at the table, determined to complete his task. However the persistent smell returned, at once fragrant and over-powering. "I got disgusted with it at that point" Mike says, "so I got the paperwork done and went upstairs to copy the forms and get away from that damn smell." However, the smell and whatever was causing it, would not be so easily dispelled.

"I was upstairs about three minutes when the smell came again. It was like something was following me. I called my wife upstairs and said, 'Do you smell that?' She told me that she didn't but we got out of there pretty quick after that," Mike remembers.

Officer Richardson also tells of other encounters with the phantom presence at the school bus garage. Once, after working a long afternoon shift on a Friday, Mike arrived at the bus garage to relax for a few minutes before going on duty at a school football game that evening. Alone in the garage, Mike turned up his police radio to listen for a call and then stretched out in a comfortable chair in the driver's lounge, his feet propped up on the table before him.

"I was tired, because it had been a long day and I was trying hard to stay awake because if you miss a call, it is your butt. But I was just sort of drifting off a little when I felt someone push my foot. It was gentle but it was definite. It was like someone was either playing with me or just trying to help me stay awake." If the latter was the purpose, it worked because Mike was immediately riveted to wide-eyed attention.

Interestingly, Officer Richardson does not seem to feel threatened or frightened by the presence he has encountered in the area of the high school. Instead, he seems to feel that whatever spirit may linger there has developed an affinity for him.

"Maybe she likes it there," he muses. "Maybe she likes me! This is such a female dominated environment, from the teachers to the bus drivers and then you get a tall burly guy like me in here....If you buy the idea that this is a child's ghost, a little girl... maybe I feel safe to her. My experiences are tantamount to a child coming up and poking you to get your attention. Maybe she just wants my attention, that's all."

If so, then she has gotten it. In fact, on at least one occasion, Officer Richardson believes she might have even tried to "reach out and touch" him via the bus garage phone system.

"I have had one phone call. When we go into the upstairs office in the bus garage, there is a telephone system with rows of buttons. One of those buttons is for an interoffice intercom. If you press the button, the person on the other end can see what office you are buzzing from because the button lights up.

"One night I was up in the secretary's office, about ready to phone in a report, when the phone started ringing. It was an odd, weak-sounding ring and when I looked down I could see that it was the intercom and that it was coming from the garage. I knew I was alone in the building, but I picked it up anyway and there was no one there."

No one there...perhaps.

Other stories from within the bus garage abound. One staff member has reported the sound of a child's cough coming from thin air immediately behind them when they worked in the garage. Also, staff and local authorities were bewildered by a series of fire alarms that sounded from the building one day several years ago. Though the alarm system had never exhibited any errant behavior previously, suddenly all of the alarms went off several times in succession one morning. Police and fire officials were called, but no fire was present and though alarm inspectors examined through the system carefully, no explanation could be found.

Finally, after about two hours, the fire detectors ceased their erratic behavior and fire personnel left, no doubt with a sigh of relief. Their relief was premature, however, because several hours later they were called back to the garage. Once again the alarms had been set off by an unseen source. Again the system was checked and no equipment failure found. It should be noted that since that day the alarms have never again exhibited such odd behavior.

Despite all those who have reported experiences with whatever presence haunts the bus garage, it has fallen only to two people to actually glimpse the specter. Both of these have been night custodians working in the high school.

One of these is Betty Graebeck*, a pleasant, middle-aged custodian who has worked at the school for a number of years. Interestingly, when she started working there, she had never heard the tales of the young girl's death and was unaware of the ghostly tales told of the place. All of that abruptly changed, however, late one evening about seven years ago.

"It was late–about 10:30 or so and I was in the hall leading to the auditorium," Ms. Graebeck recalls. "I was walking down the hall to go back to the area where I had been working when this girl came running past me. Sometimes kids do come back late from events and get dropped off at school so I did not think too much about it. However, there were a couple of things that were strange about her. The first thing I noticed was that she was barefoot. I thought 'Now that is odd.' Then I noticed she had a short-sleeved dress on and that seemed odd too because it was early winter."

Ms. Graebeck describe the girl as about fourteen or fifteen, with long blond hair and a pretty face, wearing a long white dress.

"As she passed me, I said 'hello!' and the girl just smiled at me and ran past me down the hall. It was strange but I just thought that the bus had dropped her off from some late club event and she was going to her locker. But then, about twenty minutes alter, she ran past me again!"

Somewhat puzzled by her experience, Ms. Graebeck went to her superior the next day and hesitatingly told him of her observations.

"I said to him, 'You are not going to believe what I saw last night,' " Betty began. "I told him that there was this girl running the halls with no shoes on, but before I could go on, he stopped me and said, 'Wait a minute. Did she have long blond hair and a white dress?' I said to him, 'Have you seen her too?' He said no, but others had and then told me, 'She is that ghost that has been in here before.' Then he went on to tell me about the death of that girl."

At least one other custodian has reported seeing the fleeting form of a girl in a long while dress traipsing through the empty halls of the school late at night. According to Betty Graebeck, the worker in question swore that he had saw the form of the girl glide past him in a hallway one night and then pass directly through a pair of closed and locked doors at the end of the hall. The phantom of the high school was taking her nightly stroll.

The stories persist to this day. From student to student, staff member to staff member, tales are told and retold, perhaps embellished with each retelling. Beneath the veneer of such stories, however, lies a undeniable truth: in the halls of this educational facility, like some others in Indianapolis and across the nation, something enigmatic may walk–something that defies explanation or comprehension. Something that, some would argue, should best be left dead and buried, yet refuses to lie quiet.

In the end, perhaps it is best described by Officer Richardson, who reflects:

"Maybe it is a sad thing. Maybe it is a lost soul or something... I don't know. It is not something I presume to understand, but the one thing that bothers me in all this is...it is there. Whatever or whoever it is, *it is there*."

4
The Spirit of Mercy
St. Joseph Community Hospital
Mishawaka, Indiana

Whenever the subject of ghosts is discussed, sooner or later the question arises as to why the spirits of the living are said to return after death. The possible motivations for a spirit to return to the land of the living has been the subject of speculation by folklorists and parapsychologists for many years. Curiously, most of the reasons attributed to spirits are distinctly negative. The "typical" ghost is said to return due to the tragic or traumatic nature of its death, perhaps due to some business left unfinished in life, or even to wreak vengeance on the living for a past grievance. Such unfortunate incentives for returning from the grave tend to make for stories of unhappy, malevolent specters.

However, in compiling such a list of possible motives for a spirit to return to the location of their former life, one motive is often missed. Some ghosts are said to return for positive reasons, such as to express compassion, concern, or even love.

This might be made more understandable if you remember that ghosts, if they exist, are the reflections of the life that they once led. As Troy Taylor, president of the American Ghost Society has said:

> "What people have to understand is that conscious, intelligent spirits are really just left-over personalities of people who once lived. We all have personalities that make us what we are. Those who were weak or angry in life will be the same in death... just as those who were kind and compassionate in life will also be the same way as a disembodied spirit. No one really understands just what the "personality" or "soul" really

is... if we can't prove that it exists inside of our body, who is to say that it cannot exist outside?"

This is to suggest that spirits said to walk the earth may simply be echoes of their former personalities. If this is the case, then it would go far toward explaining the rare tales of kind, benevolent ghosts which abound throughout our state.

Such is the case of the spectral nun said to have once walked the floors of a wing at St. Joseph Community Hospital in Mishawaka. Far from being the angry or vengeful phantom commonly portrayed in ghost stories, this spirit is said, by those who claim to have encountered her, to be a kind, gentle soul, seeking only to bring comfort and solace to those enduring difficult circumstances.

St. Joseph Community Hospital stands today as a remarkable example of the best of what a hometown general hospital can be. Far from the huge, sterile monoliths that are common of our medical institutions today, St. Joseph Hospital is a small, 126-bed facility that provides a level of personal attention and individual care sometimes impossible in larger, more specialized medical centers. Fully equipped to handle cases ranging from minor surgery to emergency care, St. Joseph Community is truly a general hospital, meeting the needs of its community with compassion and care.

Compassion and personal attention have been an integral part of the mission of St. Joseph from its earliest beginnings. The hospital traces its origins to 1878, when three Sisters from the Order of the Poor Handmaids of Jesus Christ came to northern Indiana to bring a ministry of caring for the sick. Their order, which was begun in 1851 by Mother Mary Kasper, specialized in bringing nursing care to the areas where they ministered, particularly to the poor and indigent. Here they found a need and an appreciation for their efforts. The Sisters quickly moved in, established the St. Agnes Convent, and began their ministry.

As early pioneers in the field that is now called Home Health Care, these tireless women spent their days and nights caring for residents of the area, giving of their loving care without recompense. Records indicate that in 1879, forty-four sick persons were cared for and the nuns had spent seventy-nine nights "watching at the bedsides of the sick."

At times, patients were brought to the St. Agnes Convent in Mishawaka for emergency care, but as Mishawaka continued to grow, it became widely recognized that a more formal hospital setting was necessary. While today Mishawaka is an easy commute from several hospitals in the greater South Bend area, in the early 1900's such a drive was often difficult, particularly for the elderly and infirm. As an article of the time from the *Mishawaka Enterprise* relates, "That Mishawaka has long needed a local hospital is a self-evident fact."

Consequently, in 1906, a group of area physicians and business leaders approached the Sisters with a request that they spearhead an effort to build an inpatient hospital in the town. Fundraising in the community was met with great enthusiasm and success and on June 14, 1909, ground was broken for St. Joseph Community Hospital. Less than ten months later the hospital was officially opened with forty beds and a staff of five Sisters serving as nurses.

With the growth of Mishawaka in the succeeding decades, the hospital also grew, with at least eight major renovations or additions being completed, the most recent in 1993. The passing years have brought new staff and programs to the hospital, yet the emphasis on Christian service and personal care has remained. This philosophy, a legacy of the selfless Sis-

Photo: St. Joseph Hospital Archives Department

The original St. Joseph Community Hospital in Mishawaka, Indiana.

ters who founded this venerable institution, has guided the work of St. Joseph Hospital for nearly a hundred years. Indeed, it can be said that the spirit of the nuns who gave their lives to the ministry of the hospital lives on there.

Such a statement might well be more literally true than one would imagine, if the stories which have quietly developed there over the years are to be believed. For, it is said, at least one such nun who gave her life caring for the sick in the hospital has remained there many years after her demise.

Throughout the years of the hospital's existence, the Poor Handmaids of Jesus Christ has maintained ownership of the institution. While today the active role of the Sisters at St. Joseph Hospital is limited to fulfilling three administrative positions, in the past these dedicated nuns served in many capacities, from nursing staff to chaplaincy work on the wards. Significantly, for decades, a few nuns actually lived on the wards in order to be available at all times to the patients who might need them. These women gave their lives to caring for the sick and comforting families, bringing solace and a sense of peace to those in desperate circumstances. One of these nuns is said to have stayed on duty, long after her mortal existence has ended.

Just ask Kevin Geisel. A native of Mishawaka, Kevin is a gregarious, down-to-earth businessman. Interestingly, Mr. Geisel grew up attending a Catholic elementary school in the area. "I grew up around nuns," he says with a grin, "and believe me, I know what a nun looks like." When Kevin left parochial school to attend a public high school, no doubt he thought his close association with nuns was at an end. However, on at least one occasion, Kevin would encounter a Sister in circumstances that were strange, to say the least.

In April 1993 Kevin was admitted to St. Joseph Community Hospital for abdominal surgery. "I had surgery on a Friday morning and, amazingly, by that night I did not have much pain at all," he now recalls. "The doctor took away the pain medication on Saturday and told me that if I needed anything for pain. I could ask the nurse for something, but I really was pain-free. As a matter of fact, by Saturday I was up and walking."

Actually, the only problem that Kevin encountered those first few days after surgery was the boredom that often accompanies patients in a hospital who are feeling well. "I was not used to all that rest," Kevin says, "so by Saturday night I was up walking the hallways talking to the nurses. About midnight I decided to go back to my room and try and get some sleep. I was lying there awake in my bed when in came this nun.

"She was older, at least over fifty, and fairly short. She was wearing glasses and I noticed right away that she was wearing one of the older habits with the white band across the forehead, like the nuns used to wear when I was growing up. She came into the open doorway of my room and just sort of stood there. I could see her clearly in the light from the hallway. Sometimes nurses will come in at night and ask you if they can get you anything, or if you want a back rub to help you get to sleep and I thought that she was going to ask me something like that, but she didn't. She just stood there in the doorway for a couple of minutes, looking at me, and then she left. There was nothing frightening or eerie about her being there and I assumed that she was just a nun from the hospital checking up on me."

Perhaps, as Mr. Geisel conjectures, the Sister was doing just that. However, he was shortly to learn something shocking regarding the nature of his late night visitor. "Not too much later," Kevin remembers, "a nurse came into my room to ask me if I needed anything. I told her I was having trouble sleeping and asked if she could give me something to help me sleep. Then I asked who the Sister was who had been in and the nurse got kind of a funny look on her face. Then she told me that there were no nuns on the surgical floor."

When Kevin assured her that a nun had been in his room just a few minutes before, the nurse sat down and gently told Kevin a strange story. She reported to Kevin that many years before, a nun had lived in an area adjacent to the surgical floor. It was her job to help care for the patients who were recovering from surgery and she had done so faithfully until her death several decades before. "She told me that since her death, the nun had periodically been seen by patients and staff on the fifth floor surgical wing, just checking in on patients. I thought that was awesome, but then I do not scare very easily," Kevin adds.

Despite the fact that Mr. Geisel would stay in the hospital several more days, this would be the last time he would glimpse the phantom nun. Others, however, have reported her presence there for many years. Janice

Harper,* a retired nurse who worked on the surgical floor at St. Joseph for more than ten years recalls several instances when patients claimed to have encountered the ghost.

"No one at the hospital ever spoke of it much, but occasionally we on the floor staff would hear about her being around," she remembers with a smile. "I came to work at St. Joseph in 1972 and it was about four years later that I started working on the surgery floor. I mostly worked the day shift, but sometimes I would work nights and that tended to be the time when you would hear about her.

"We nurses are known to be practical, no-nonsense types, and working on a surgical floor you get to be all business, so naturally no one talked about a ghost on the floor when I started working there. I would have thought someone was nuts if they had told me something like that."

Her attitude changed one night several months after she began work on the floor. Entering the room of a patient scheduled for surgery the next day, Janice was surprised to find the patient sitting up in bed, despite the late hour. "I asked him if he was nervous about his surgery and if he needed something to help him sleep. Rather cheerily, the man told me no, that he felt relaxed and fine since praying with the nun who had come in a few minutes before. I was surprised at that since, even then, we had only a few nuns working at the hospital and none of them would be likely to be visiting patients on the floor at 2 A.M. He asked me who she was since she had not introduced herself and he was afraid he might have offended her by not asking for her name. I told him I did not know but I would check with the other nurses to see if they could tell me."

"After checking his medications, I left the room and returned to the nurse station where a couple of the nurses and our supervisor were sitting drinking coffee. I asked them if we had a chaplain on duty and they told me that there might be, but they had not seen one on the floor that night. Then I told them what the gentleman had told me about praying with a nun and how he was afraid that he might have offended her by not asking for her name. I can remember my supervisor's eyes getting really wide and she said to me, 'Are you sure he was not putting you on?' When I told them that he was sincere, the head nurse looked at one of the other nurses there and said, 'Well, I guess the Sister is back!' "

Unsure how to interpret this strange reaction, Mrs. Harper repeated to her coworkers what the man had told her and asked them again if they knew who the Sister was. "You can tell him that he needn't worry about offending her," came the reply from an older nurse in the group. "She is not really alive and I think she is *way* past being offended." Then the nursing supervisor told her matter-of-factly of the elderly nun who had lived for so many years just a few feet from the surgical floor and how, since her death, she had since been seen repeatedly in patients' rooms.

"I started to get real spooked at that point," Janice recalls, "but the nurse told me not to worry because she was a nice spirit. She had never really frightened anyone and in fact, all she seemed to want was to help the patients. I thought about that for a few minutes and I started to feel better. Then I went back to work."

This, however, would not be the last that Mrs. Harper would hear of the gentle phantom who was said to share her concern for the patients' well being. On several other occasions, she spoke to patients who claimed to have encountered the benevolent phantom.

"It did not happen often," she says, "and I would not say it happened on a regular basis, but sometimes a patient or family member would tell you that they had seen her walking the halls or coming in the rooms to

Photo: St. Joseph Hospital Archives Department

The original staff of St. Joseph Community Hospital at a groundbreaking ceremony in 1909.

check on them. Mostly she was silent; however, sometimes she would pray with the patient or offer comfort to the family member watching by the bedside."

One such occurrence stands out in her memory vividly. "It was in the late seventies and it was one of those wild spring nights. There was thunder and lightning flashing all around outside and none of the patients could sleep. We were on our feet all night that night, dispensing sleeping pills and checking on the patients. In one room at the far end of the hall, there was an older gentleman who was in for surgery on a broken hip and he had been in pain for several days. About midnight I went into check on him and I was delighted to find him resting comfortably for the first time in days.

"His eyes were closed and so, thinking that he was sleeping, I turned to tiptoe out of the room when he looked up at me and told me that he did not think he would be needing any pain medication that night. I told him that was great and I was glad he was feeling better. He smiled and said, 'I think the nun that was in here took all the pain with her when she left.' As soon as he said that my heart skipped a beat."

Janice was about to ask the man what he meant, but at that moment she heard a call coming from the other end of the hall, so, wishing the man a good night, she quickly left. She was intrigued, however, and before her shift ended Mrs. Harper went back to the elderly gentleman's room to talk to him further. By now it was several hours later, but she found that he was still lying peacefully, apparently without pain. Remarking how glad she was that his pain was better, the man flatly said, "I told you, the Sister you sent in took the pain away!"

The man said he had been in great pain the night before and could not lie comfortably in any position. At about midnight he had slipped off into an uneasy sleep. When he awoke a short time later, he was surprised to see an elderly nun standing at his bedside, her head bent in an attitude of prayer. "There was something comforting in having her there," the elderly patient told Janice, "and after a minute she reached out and held my hand. Her hand was cold, but when she touched me, I felt very relaxed for the first time in a week. Then the pain gradually began to fade from my hip and leg. In a minute all that was left was a dull ache. She looked down at me and smiled and then walked out of the room without a word."

"She went out into the hall?" Janice asked on a whim.

"Yes, she left by the door, but the funny thing is... I never saw the door open when she left!" the man added.

Mrs. Harper goes on to explain that she is reluctant to say that the patient in question was "healed" by the presence of the phantom Sister. However, she says, "Whatever it was that he saw did bring a sense of peace and relaxation to that man's body. Sometimes just the act of relaxing helps to ease pain and so who am I to question what he experienced?"

As strange as such incidents might seem, in the busy world of a surgical ward they were paid little attention. "We did not think about it much," Janice says, "because we had other things that consumed our time. But every so often one of the nurses would say that a patient had reported seeing her or if something was misplaced from the desk, someone would joke that the Sister had taken it. No one really wanted to talk about it much because in a hospital setting, the idea of a ghost is not exactly encouraged. Still, most of us knew she was there."

Indeed, while many longtime employees at St. Joseph say they have never heard of the legend of the ghostly nun, a few who worked in and around the fifth floor surgical ward acknowledge that they have heard the stories. At least one former maintenance worker there even claims to have caught a fleeting glimpse of her.

The worker in question, who was often called upon to do routine maintenance on the floor, recounts standing on a ladder in the hallway replacing fluorescent lighting one night when he glanced down to see a dark form gliding past him. "I only caught a quick glimpse of whatever it was," he now says, "because it turned the corner at the end of the hall just a few feet in front of me. But I remember when I saw the figure, my first thought was to wonder what the heck a nun was doing on the floor after visiting hours. She looked like she was dressed in the old, flowing habits they used to wear years ago."

Curious about the identity of the woman, the worker climbed down from his ladder and followed her path into the adjacent hallway. When he got there, however, the hallway was empty. "I could not have been more than ten steps behind her," he remarks, "but when I got there the hallway was empty. A minute later, one of the nurses came by and saw me standing there and asked me if there was a problem. When I told her I was looking for a nun, she stared at me kind of strange and then said that there were no nuns on the floor. Then she said 'At least, no live ones.' It was only a few years later that I heard the story of the ghost on the surgical floor."

It is interesting to note that this is apparently the only report of a worker seeing the fleeting form of the spectral Sister. Instead, reports of her presence seem to have come almost exclusively from patients in the surgical ward and, occasionally, from their families as well. An example of the latter comes from Jennifer Rowell, an elderly widow who lives in Mishawaka. Her experience with the ghostly nun came nearly fifteen years ago when her husband, Jim, was a patient at St. Joseph.

"Jim had been in the hospital several times," she recalls, "with different surgeries to fix a heart problem. The last of his surgeries was going to be the most extensive and when we checked into the hospital the night before the surgery, Jim was pretty upset. I stayed with him till late and then went home for a couple of hours of sleep.

"When I got back there the next morning, Jim told me that he had had a wonderful dream the night before that a nun had come into his room and prayed beside his bed. I did not think much about it. Jim and I were both Methodist and why he would dream about a nun did not make much sense but he seemed to think of it as a positive dream, so I let it go at that."

Mrs. Rowell goes on to relate that the surgery that day was a long one and when her husband was wheeled back into his room that evening, the prognosis was guarded at best. "The surgery had not gone as they expected," she says, "and Jim had lost a great deal of blood. When they wheeled him in he was pale and cold to the touch and there were machines and tubes all over him. The doctor had told me that I should stay the night because they were not totally sure that he would make it, so I just sat there in his room holding his hand and crying. Eventually I fell asleep sitting in the chair next to the bed, holding his hand."

Exactly when Mrs. Rowell was aawkened she cannot say, except that it was well into the early morning hours. "It was still dark outside," she remembers, "and the only light in the room was from the lamp next to his bed. Somehow I woke up with this strong feeling that there was someone else in the room. I expected to see a nurse, but when I turned I saw this short nun standing there quietly in the corner of the room.

Immediately I remembered Jim's dream from the night before and thought that maybe someone had really come in to pray with him. I could not see much of her face in the dim light but before I could say anything, she kind of gently whispered, 'He will live. Everything will be all right'. And, strangely, in that moment, I thought that it would. I had hope for the first time in months. I glanced down at Jim for a second and when I turned back to thank the Sister for her kind words, she was gone–just that quick. I had not heard any footsteps or anything."

Jennifer's husband did indeed recover from his surgery and with the help of the doctors and nurses at St. Joseph, he went on to live another ten years. Moreover, for the rest of his life, Jim Rowell was fond of recounting the story of his ghostly bedside visitor and the peace and healing she had brought.

So the legends go at St. Joseph. The hospital itself seems to take little stock in the tales of a spectral nun who was said to walk the floors of the surgical ward. In recent years the fifth floor has been renovated and now serves as offices for the hospital administration. No further reports concerning the phantom presence have been heard since, and if the gentle spirit of a compassionate Sister does still walk there, one might only guess at her reaction to finding office desks and copy machines where once she tended the needs of the sick.

Those who know the stories best, however, tend to think that she is no longer present on the fifth floor of the hospital. It may be, with the passing of the old surgical ward, the spirit herself may have passed on to better things as well. As Janice Harper remarks,

> As crazy as it sounds, those of us who worked around the stories always thought of the spirit fondly. She was not some spooky ghost out of the movies dragging chains and moaning. She was a kind spirit, who apparently only wanted to comfort and help the patients. That is the way she had spent her life and so maybe she just continued doing so after her death. But I would like to think that now that she is no longer needed, she has finally gone to her reward... after all those years, maybe she has gone off duty.

5
The Historic Haunts of Knox County
Knox County, Indiana

Knox County, Indiana, may well boast of being one of the most historic areas in Indiana and perhaps the Midwest. Originally incorporated on June 20, 1793, at the behest of the first regional governor, Winthrop Sargent, Knox County has been labeled "the mother of all counties." Indeed, when chartered, the county encompassed an area that stretched from the Miami River to the east, to the Ohio River to the south, and north all the way into what is now Canada. This includes much of the land that is now Indiana, Ohio, Illinois and Michigan.

To this vast wilderness inhabited only by French fur trappers, Native Americans and a few hardy settlers, Governor Sargent appointed John Small as the first Knox County sheriff. It was his job to bring law and a sense of civility to this rugged region. It was also his daunting task to (in the words of a later historian) "organize a complete county government for these poor, ignorant French peasants who were better acquainted with the manorial government of the middle ages than that of the English county." [1]

As time passed and the middle section of the continent slowly became settled, the boundaries of Knox County were whittled down. In 1805, the territory of Michigan was taken from it and the territory of Illinois was separated in 1809. In 1800, when Indiana was declared an official territory, Vincennes, the county seat of Knox County, was named its territorial capital.

Vincennes itself, the first settlement in Indiana, was originally settled in about 1732 by the French, primarily to aid them in the fur trade. The king of France named Francois Morgane de Vincennes as the first commandant of the settlement at the time of its inception and by 1752, the post had appropriated his name. In 1760, Vincennes was taken over by the British after the French and Indian War. During the American Revolution, American Commander George Rogers Clark made a daring capture of the fort, only to lose it again shortly thereafter to the British forces .[2]

Long after the Americans gained control of the area, however, the populous of the region was still primarily made up of French and Canadians, with an intermingling of American Indian, and Spanish cultures. Through the years, Vincennes and Knox County in general have been stirred into the melting pot of American culture, yet still the old world influence can be felt.

Today, Knox County is a wonderful mixture of old and new. Vincennes is a town of about 20,000 people that still maintains a subtle flavor of its historic past. Much of the rest of the county, though, still retains an atmosphere of rural gentility and quiet serenity. In this oldest settled area in the state, the past and present seem to be interwoven in a delicate balance.

The area is at once beautiful and historic, a place where the rich texture of tradition and the lore of bygone days are very much a part of the cultural heritage. It should not be surprising, then, that this heritage should include a great many spots said to be frequented by ghosts and spirits of a long past era.

Richard King, a local historian and folklore researcher, has made it his avocation to collect this more eerie side of Knox County history, making this fascinating information available to the public through his website, "A Haunted Tour of Knox County"[3]. Through his efforts, as well as that of other local historians and folklorists, this collection of ghostly legends has been preserved.

Donna Mariana, the Crying Spirit of Otter Lake

If one were to begin a tour of the haunted places of Knox County, a good starting point would be Otter Lake, a sleepy locale about one mile south if Vincennes.

Sitting by its tranquil waters, dappled by sunlight filtering through the trees on a fall afternoon, it is easy to think of this as a place of peace and rustic serenity. However, as the waves gently lap against the shore and the breeze rustles the leaves, it is said that if one listens closely enough, a eerie sound can be heard – a song, or perhaps a soft moan, seeming to come at once from a great distance and yet from very near. The old and wise ones say it is the mournful cry of Donna Mariana, lamenting her lost love and a life cut short centuries ago.

The story of Donna Mariana Gonzales reaches back a great many years to the early settlement in Vincennes, when there was, among the French populous, a small Spanish contingent living in the area. According to the old legend, one of the more prosperous and well regarded of the Spanish families was that of Don Samon Gonzales. Don Samon came from a proud family heritage in Spain and when he settled in the rural precincts of southern Indiana, he brought with him both wealth and traditional family pride. His was one of the most opulent estates in the area, with a large home and many servants. Yet his greatest prize on earth was his beautiful daughter, Donna Mariana.

Donna Mariana had been born in Indiana, yet had been reared in the finest Spanish style. By the time she reached the age of sixteen, she had blossomed into one of the most beautiful and elegant young women in the area. It was only natural, then, that many young men of the region would take a great interest in the girl. However, the stern Don Samon took a dim view of these locals as unsuitable, vowing instead that he would arrange a marriage more fitting his daughter's station in life.

Still, the wonders of young love, like any other force of nature, cannot be long contained. Despite (or perhaps because of) her father's strict admonitions, Donna Mariana met and fell in love with a handsome young local name Duffee. The relationship was doomed from the beginning since the young man, though honest and hard working, was well below the station in life accorded Donna Mariana, as well as being from French extraction. In reality the young woman knew that she could never gain her father's approval for the match.

Still, as time wore on, her love for the young man burned within her and Donna Mariana began to slip away on summer evenings to meet her lover by the serene beauty of nearby Otter Lake. There, under the summer moon, the two would look into each others eyes and dare to dream of a life together that each secretly knew they would never share.

Sometimes on long warm afternoons, Donna Mariana and her beau, accompanied by other young men and women of the area, would be found on the waters of Otter lake, boating and fishing. During these times, the pair tried desperately not to show the nature of their feelings for one another, fearing the consequences should their secret become public knowledge. Yet such depth of feeling cannot be long hidden and soon rumors of their love affair began to circulate through the community.

One day these rumors came to the attention of Don Samon, who predictably flew into a rage and confronted his daughter. The distraught young girl did not have the courage to deny the truth and in no uncertain terms her father insisted that she never see Duffee again. Within days, the full extent of his dictate became apparent when Don Samon announced to his daughter that she would be leaving in a few weeks to go to St. Genevieve, a Spanish settlement on the west bank of the Mississippi. There, she was to wed to an older Spanish gentleman of means and proper aristocratic birth. Heartbroken, the delicate Donna Mariana met this news with sobs and pathetic pleadings, yet nothing she could say could move her father's heart.

As the time of her departure grew closer, the once beautiful and vivacious girl grew sullen and withdrawn. Her beautiful dark eyes that had once seemed to dance with merriment became dull and lifeless and she was seen no more in town, or at the gatherings of her former friends. The young Duffee, upon learning of the fate of his beloved, rode to her home and demanded entrance, but was turned away by her father. Armed with a sword, Don Samon swore to him that as long as they both drew breath, the pair would never be together. He was, perhaps, more accurate than he knew.

As the date of her departure came and went, the young people of the community mourned the loss of their pretty companion, but none more so than Duffee. Soon after Donna Mariana had apparently been forced to take leave to St. Genevieve, a few of Duffee's friends, attempting to roust him from his gloom, coaxed him into an afternoon hunting expedition on the shores of Otter Lake.

It is said that as the young men trudged the shores of the lake, searching for game, a mournful cry floated across the waters to their ears. So distinct was the sound that the party stopped to listen. After a few moments the sound faded into silence and one of the young men suggested that it had merely been the cry of a loon. Unconvinced, the band resumed their rambles.

A short distance further along the shore, however, one of the hunters happened to glance into the water and was stopped cold in his tracks once again. Before him was a horrifying sight. From just below the surface of the still, clear water, a beautiful face peered up at him–its dark eyes open, fixed in death. Horrified, the young man called this sight to the attention of the rest of the group. Young Duffee, recognizing the face before him frantically plunged into the water and, aided by his compatriots, brought forth the lifeless body of young Donna Mariana.

Clearly now the true fate of the young girl became known. Instead of accepting the dictate of her father and spending her life as the wife of a proper gentleman she did not love, Donna Mariana had chosen to end her life in the cold waters of Otter Lake. Late on the night before her scheduled departure to St. Genevieve, she had slipped from her home and made her way to the lake, throwing herself in. Her father, unsure of what had transpired and too proud to publicize the fact of his daughters disappearance, had sent servants to search for her. When it became apparent that the search was in vain, he had thrown up his hands and ceased his efforts to locate his daughter. A tragic victim of a cruel fate, the body of Donna Mariana was taken to her father's home and quietly interred in a family cemetery nearby.

Still, over the passing decades and centuries, her legend has lived on. Hunters and fishermen traveling in the area of Otter Lake have reported that often late at night a melancholy sound has floated over the water toward them. Some describe it as a haunting song; others say it is a low moan of anguish and despair. The wise ones say that it is Donna Mariana crying for her lost love and crying her despair at her fate.

A few fishermen have even said that if you peer into the waters of Otter Lake intently, you will sometimes see a beautiful face peering up at you through dark eyes–eyes that once danced with laughter, but now are clouded over in death. It is, they say, the face of Donna Mariana, reminding the world of her tragic fate in the serene waters of Otter Lake.

The Girl on the Tracks and the
Purple Head of Stangle's Bridge

For some reason, bridges have long been noted as sites of weird tales and ghostly occurrences. Perhaps there is something about their vast expanses and often isolated locations that make these structures ideal as settings for ghostly stories. Perhaps, as the ancients believed, there is something about crossing over running water that acts as a magnet for supernatural disturbances.

Whatever the cause, several bridges in Indiana have been known to reportedly host spectral inhabitants. The area around Knox County can boast of not one but two distinct haunted bridges within its boundaries.

The first such tale is concerns a railroad trestle over the Embarrass River, just ten miles west of Vincennes, just as it crosses over the border into Illinois. Indeed, the bridge in question lies just over the border from Indiana, yet due to its proximity to the Hoosier state, it has become part of Knox County folklore, and hence is included in this collection. Owned today by the CSX Transportation Corporation, the bridge was operated for many years by the B&O Railroad, which supplied freight and passenger service between nearby Lawrenceville, Illinois, and Vincennes.

The origin of the tale of the girl on the tracks, as she is known, is uncertain. One of the legends suggests that she was a local girl who grew up in one of the small nearby villages during the first decades of this century. The pretty young girl is said to have been engaged to be married to her childhood sweetheart, but before their planned wedding date the young man was called to service in the army during World War I. Like many other young couples of the time, they bade each other a tearful goodbye, with the young soldier promising to come home and marry her "when Johnny came marching home."

It was a promise he would never be given the opportunity to fulfill. A year after his departure, the young man's letters suddenly stopped arriving and shortly thereafter came the official notification that the girl's worst fears had been realized: her fiancé had lost his life in the muddy trenches of France.

The girl was frantic in her grief. Neither friends nor family could console her, nor could they conceive of the awful plan that was developing in her thoughts. Her shock and grief slowly giving way to madness, the young girl made a foolhardy and fatal decision. Late one evening she went to her hope chest and removed the wedding dress she had placed there many months ago. Preparing herself as though for her wedding day, the girl next slipped unnoticed from her house and walked the several miles to the railroad bridge over the Embarrass River. There she waited patiently for her appointment with death and her hoped-for reunion with her betrothed

At eleven o'clock, as a shrill whistle in the distance announced the approach of a freight train bound for Vincennes, the girl mounted the railroad trestle and slowly walked to the midpoint of the expanse. As the train thundered nearer, the girl quietly stepped onto the tracks.

It is said that the engineer did not see the girl until she was directly in front of his locomotive. So fast was the train speeding through the night that he had no opportunity to stop before hearing the dull thud of her body against the engine. When he was able to stop the train some quarter mile down the tracks, all that could be found of the girl was a smear of blood along the side of the engine and a scrap of white lace from her wedding dress.

It should be noted that other legends of the girl's demise abound in the surrounding community. Some say that she was a war bride from World War II. Some say she was a teenager who committed suicide for no apparent reason. Since historical archives of the event do not exist, the real truth will never be truly known.

However, one thing is certain: since that day, legends say that many engineers and operators of the railway have seen her spirit. Time and again, just as their trains crossed the midway point of the bridge over the Embarrass River, engineers have been horrified to see the shape of a young girl in a long white dress step from the darkness of the bridge directly into the path of their oncoming locomotive. A few have sworn they even have heard the sound of her body as it collided with the engine, but after hastily stopping the train, no body could be found.

Some engineers and brakemen have even told grisly stories of watching as the young girl was caught under the wheels of the locomotive and seeing a flash of blood as they passed. In time, as radios were added to the trains, engineers are said to have frantically radioed back to the caboose of their trains, asking brakemen there if they had seen anything as they passed, but nothing has ever been seen. According to legend, these tragic reenactments always occurred late at night and always to trains bound from Vincennes.

According to rumors, so frequent were these occurrences that the railroad office ordered engineers never to stop on that stretch of railway, even if they thought they had hit someone standing in the tracks. Moreover, workmen were ordered never to speak of these strange encounters on penalty of forfeiting their jobs.

Yet the legend lives on. Even today it is said that as trains thunder out of the night to cross the bridge over the Embarrass River, those on board strain their eyes against the darkness, fearful that they might see the spectral shape of a pretty young woman in a long white dress step into the path of their train just as she has for over eighty years.

As eerie as this ghostly presence along the CSX railway bridge might be, she is not the only specter said to haunt a bridge in Knox County. Over the Wabash River bottoms stretches a forlorn bridge bearing the name of Stangle's Bridge that is said to be inhabited by an eerie presence who makes himself known in some rather bizarre ways.

The bridge itself was built in the late 1800s and served for many years for railway traffic between St. Francisville and Vincennes. In the middle part of this century, the bridge was abandoned and was purchased by the Stangle family. In the early 1870s, the Stangle family converted the bridge into a toll bridge when ferry service across the Wabash River was closed and a connection was needed to Illinois.

Rarely crossed today, the bridge shows signs of its hundred-year use and stands forlorn and decrepit. However, when the mist rises and moonlight glimmers across the water beneath, it is said that this bridge is also the domain of an unearthly presence.

Several stories are told to explain the apparition that has periodically appeared for years along the expanse of Stangle's Bridge. Some say that is the spirit of James Johnston, a local hero of the Revolutionary War, whose farm once stood along the shore that abuts the bridge. It was there, some one hundred and eighty years ago, that Johnston was laid to rest in a family plot overlooking the Wabash. Some whisper that Johnston, who was active in founding Vincennes, rises from his grave to search for those who trespass on the land he once owned.

Another story commonly told in the area is that the spirit is that of a Catholic priest who, one cold December night, fell from a train crossing the bridge toward St. Francisville. The Rev. J.B. Hatter, pastor of the St. Francisville Catholic Church, had been to Vincennes that evening to attend some Christmas festivities and, traveling back toward his home, became ill in the passenger compartment of the train. Stepping out onto the platform between cars for fresh air, the priest was thrown from the train when it took a sudden lurch, in the process hitting his head on the bridge abutment. He was transported to a local home, where he died a few hours later.

Perhaps the most fascinating story of the spirit of Stangle's Bridge, however, traces its origins to the early days of the settlement of Vincennes. In those days, the violence so common between settlers and Native Americans flared in the community. A contingent of Indians is said to have fought a brief but bloody skirmish with settlers along the banks of the Wabash near the spot where Stangle's Bridge now stands. During the skirmish the shaman, or medicine man, of the tribe was killed, his body falling from the banks into the river. Before his fellow tribesmen could retrieve his body, it was swept away by the swirling water, never to be recovered.

Indian belief specifies that in order for a spirit to have peace, it must receive a proper burial. Furthermore, moving water was considered abhorrent to spirits and so it was said at the time that surely the shaman's spirit would not find rest.

Perhaps this is so. In any case, whoever or whatever is said to haunt the area of Stangle's Bridge has been whispered about for many years. It is not so much the identity of the spirit that has made it famous in the community as it is that manner of its appearance. It is said that, crossing the span of the bridge at night, as the mist rises, one might well see a luminous purple hand reaching up toward the bridge from the water below, as though in supplication.

Those who have stopped their progress when confronted with this sight say that shortly thereafter, a bloated purple head rises to the surface of the river and floats to the side of the bridge, peering intently at them. According to local tales, this vision has been seen by many over the succeeding years and even today, though the bridge is seldom used, cars can be seen stopped on the bridge at night, waiting for the appearance of the ghastly purple head. Whether it is the spirit of an Indian shaman, an early settler, or an ill-fated cleric, its presence has become legendary to succeeding generations.

The Headless Horsewoman of Ghostly Hollow

It is dark. A chill wind that moans through claw-like branches swirls and scatters crackling, dried corpses of dead leaves. A narrow dirt road slopes down toward a hollow where the branches close in overhead, blotting out the roadway in shadowy blackness.[4]

Thus begins a 1981 *Valley Advance* newspaper description of the aptly named glen long known as "Ghostly Hollow." A little-used passage just a mile northeast of Wheatland, Indiana, the area has sadly become a recent casualty of a coal mining operation. In its time, the roadway looked much like many other rural back roads found throughout the state. However, at night, as the wind whipped through the tall trees canopying the road, casting odd shapes in the moonlight, Ghostly Hollow bore up well to its name, for it was on nights such as these that *she* was said to ride again.

Most Americans have heard the classic tale of "The Legend of Sleepy Hollow." Washington Irving's retelling of the story of the nightly romps of the famous phantom Hessian and his encounter with Ichabod Crane has been called "The classic American ghost story."

What many Hoosiers do not realize, however, is that Indiana has its own version of the classic headless horseman legend. However, what makes this tale doubly extraordinary is that the rider in this case is a horse*woman.*

Various stories are told of this ghostly rider and her nightly journeys through the Knox County countryside. One of the more persistent narratives dates back to the last years of the nineteenth century for its setting. It is the story of a high-spirited young woman named Lucy and the sad fate she met along the road that is today known as Ghostly Hollow.

According to local lore, Lucy was a crimson-haired beauty, fiery and vivacious, who was born to a farming family in the area. The youngest of six children, Lucy grew up amid the hard work and strict Protestant values common in such families. In time she grew tall and beautiful, but it was her strong will and fiery temperament that marked Lucy as unique. Far from being the docile, obedient child her parents might have wished for, Lucy, from an early age, manifested a character that was rebellious and temperamental.

Sometimes cordial, warm and loving, when crossed Lucy was known to fly into fits of rage. While she was loved by her family and friends, most who knew her sooner or later became the objects of her fury. During such fits of rage she was known to lash out at her victim with a sharp tongue, and if this did not have the desired effect, to assault them with her fists. Over time, each of her older brothers bore the bruises and bumps resulting from the ire of their youngest sister.

As she grew into young adulthood, it was Lucy's father who found himself in the most constant strife with his daughter. A stolid, practical man by nature, he could not fathom a daughter who rebelled against convention at every turn, rejecting not only his counsel but his paternal authority as well. Time and again, as night settled over the sleepy countryside, the farmhouse they shared fairly shook with the clamor of their contentious bickering.

More often than not, these altercations would end with the father throwing up his hands in helpless dismay and the daughter running from the house toward the barn and the company of her favorite horse. For, according to the old legend, Lucy was known as one of the best horseback riders in the county. While such a skill was seen by many as inappropriate for a young lady of the time, in the saddle Lucy was said to be the equal of any man.

Often, against her father's wishes, Lucy had would sneak from the farmhouse on summer afternoons to ride through the woods on her sleek black horse, her long red hair streaming behind her in the warm sun. The freedom and exhilaration of these wild rides seemed to heal her spirit and free her from the constraints of farm and family life. It was as though she was most fully alive when riding through the woods.

Sometimes, after a particularly unpleasant squabble with her father, Lucy would jump on the back of her horse and ride well into the night, not returning to her home until the first rays of dawn were painting the eastern sky. Understandably, these wild midnight rides caused a great deal of worry on the part of her parents but they were unable to contain their daughter's rebellious spirit. Moreover, as time passed, her parents realized these rides seemed to have a cleansing effect on her disposition.

Often times, after a long ride, Lucy would arrive home exhausted, yet in a cheerful frame of mind. The disagreement of the night before was forgotten and after a brief rest, her brighter spirits held sway.

It was one of those fateful disagreements, however, and Lucy's ensuing ride, that would seal her fate. Late one evening the girl came to her parents to announce that she had been invited to a small gathering of friends the next evening at a farm a few miles away. At this, her father raised an objection. The next evening was Saturday night, the evening when the family spent time together and in particular, got ready for church the next day. The old farmer solemnly proclaimed that no daughter of his would be found "gallivanting around the countryside alone on a Saturday night!"

Predictably, these words brought forth an angry response from Lucy. Harsh words were exchanged and as the rest of the family, now familiar with the customary routine, headed for their bedrooms to allow father and daughter their fracas, Lucy headed toward the door.

On this night, however, Lucy's father, driven to rage by his daughter's insolent words, chose to make a dire and ominous warning. "If you go out this night you'll not come back!" he said, his voice low and threatening. "I'll be quit of you–once and for all!" Pausing for a moment at the door, her eyes flashing brightly in the reflected firelight, Lucy stared menacingly at the old man and replied, "Fine! Then I will be gone once and for all and you will not be able to tell me what to do. You will never see me again!"

With these words, the girl was gone. In a moment she was in the barn saddling her horse, and a few minutes later her father, sitting alone, heard the sound of the horse galloping away.

Neither Lucy nor her father truly meant the bitter words they spoke that night. Despite their frequent disagreements, there was a solid core of love in their relationship. Perhaps, in other circumstances, this argument, like so many before, would have been forgotten and the relationship between daughter and father healed. However, this was not to be, for when Lucy stepped from the doorway that night, her father would never see her again . . . alive.

The night was a dark one as Lucy rode forth. Ominous clouds obscured the moon and a chill breeze brushed past her face as the horse galloped through the darkness. In the distance thunder rolled, but Lucy did not notice. Spurred by the hurt and anger burning within her, she urged her mount forward through the hollows and wooded glens she knew so well.

After riding nearly an hour, she drew back the reins and slowed her exhausted horse to a walk. Rain had started falling from the dark sky, and as it ran down her face, it mingled with the tears that had begun to well up from within. Her anger beginning to abate, she realized for the first time the gravity of her words. Clearly this night the emotional distance she had felt from her father had reached a new and terrible degree. While still unwilling to admit to herself that she had been in the wrong, as she pondered the situation one conviction became clear; she must return home. She must return and seek to mend the rift in her relationship with her father. She would go home and make peace. Lightning flashed on the path behind her and her horse reared but, heedless of the danger around her, Lucy quieted the animal, turned and began a furious gallop toward home.

No one will ever be able to know exactly what happened next. Perhaps the lightning strike had torn a branch loose, causing it to hang low over the path that Lucy knew so well. Perhaps, in her emotional upheaval, Lucy had simply forgotten that the branch was there. In any case, as she galloped forward that night, heading toward a home she would never see again, Lucy was struck in the neck by a low-hanging branch. So swift was her forward movement and so sturdy was the branch that it severed her head, which rolled off into the underbrush as the frightened steed hurdled toward home. A short distance further, her decapitated body thudded onto the path.

The next morning, an older brother, rising early for morning chores, left the farmhouse and made his way toward the barn. There, he found the riderless horse, its saddle hanging at an precarious angle, waiting by the barn door. Immediately the family was alerted and with the help of friends, they began a search of the area. It was not until well into the afternoon that a neighbor, walking the wooded glen now known as Ghostly Hollow, came upon the grisly discovery of the headless body lying in the mud of the path. A short distance further, Lucy's head was found, her red hair swirled around it in the tall grass.

His spirit broken, Lucy's father bundled the body of his daughter in a sheet and carried her back to the farmhouse. The next day she was laid to rest in a plot of earth on the farm a short distance from the horse barn. It seemed to all present that Lucy's wild midnight rides had come to an end.

However, tales told for many years afterward in the vicinity of Ghostly Hollow might well put this assumption to the test–for legend suggests that on stormy nights, when the wind blew among the trees and thunder rolled in the distance, Lucy rode again. Over the years, many who have traveled the path where she lost her life, (eventually called Ghostly Hollow) reported they were startled to hear the sudden approach of hoof beats, as of a horse furiously galloping toward them. A moment later, they related their horror at seeing a phantom black steed materialize out of the dark night, its rider headless.

In more recent years, this secluded glen became a favorite spot for teenagers, who came to park in the area and while away the hours of darkness and await their chance to see the famed headless horsewoman. With the passing of time her story has been told and retold with different variants of the tale evolving. Today, with the land around Ghostly Hollow being used for coal mining, one might well wonder if Lucy has continued her ghostly rides.

In reality, the historical veracity of the tale of Lucy, like so many old yarns, will never be truly known. However, as midnight tolls and the wind whips through the trees arching over the area once known as Ghostly Hollow, who knows but that the spirit of a strong willed, impetuous young girl might well ride again, searching for a home she never reached and seeking to mend a relationship torn by anger so many years ago. She is the headless horsewoman of Ghostly Hollow and another of the ghostly inhabitants of Knox County.

6
The Ghost Story That Never Was
Camp Chesterfield
Chesterfield, Indiana

From encounters with graveyard apparitions to hauntings at large metropolitan shopping malls, Indiana's list of ghostly tales is varied and fascinating. However, one of Indiana's most interesting ghostly tales is singular precisely because, in the end, it has no ghost. It is a humorous and ironic story of the old struggle between the magical arts community and the pseudo-religion called spiritualism. It is a story, some would argue, that speaks to the gullibility of human nature and the willingness of the unscrupulous to make a profit from feeding the human need for hope of life after death. It is the Indiana ghost story that never was.

Proponents of the movement that has come to be known as spiritualism claim to trace the origin of their "religion" back to the mysterious rites practiced by the priests of Egypt and Persia. Such a historical lineage may be a bit suspect, but it is certain that the birthplace of modern spiritualism can be traced back to a ramshackle wooden farmhouse near Hydesville, New York.

There, in 1848, the seeds of a movement that would sweep the nation and the world were sown. The events themselves began innocuously enough. In March of that year, strange knocking sounds reportedly began to be heard emanating from the bedroom of two sisters, Margaret and Kate Fox. According to the tale (which has been told and retold over the ensuing decades), their father, John, investigated the origins of the mysterious sounds but could find no apparent source. He then questioned his daughters regarding the strange noises, but they denied any knowledge of their origins, despite the fact that the knocking seemed to only occur when one or both girls were in the room.

Over the next several days, the sisters are said to have begun to make a game of communicating with whatever invisible presence was producing the knocks. At first, the girls would call out a question and ask the "spirit" (whom they named "Mr. Splitfoot") to knock once for yes and twice for no. In this way, the spirit was able to accurately answer a number of questions. Within a few days, the girls are said to have devised an elaborate code in order to allow the spirit to communicate more completely. An alphabetical code was developed, whereby a single knock would represent the letter A, two knocks the letter B and so forth. In this way, entire messages could laboriously be conveyed.

According to the old legends, through this code the spirit revealed itself to be that of a peddler who had been murdered in the house by a former owner. Some stories suggest that neighbors did recall a peddler staying at the home some years earlier, never to be seen again. Other stories state that subsequent excavation in the basement by John Fox produced a partial human skull and teeth. However, no such claims can be historically verified.

One thing is certain: the Fox sisters soon garnered considerable attention in their neighborhood through their ability to communicate with the spirit. As word of the strange events occurring at the Fox farm began to leak out into the surrounding community, neighbors gathered there each night in hopes of witnessing these bizarre "conversations." Few were disappointed.

Holding court in their sitting room, the Fox sisters would cheerfully pose questions to the spirit and before the entranced audience of neighbors and friends the spirit would tap out its spectral answers. Word continued to spread and soon crowds were flocking to the small farmhouse. Reports ran rampant concerning the strange occurrences and it was not long before the local press took notice.

In light of subsequent events, the accounts of the day regarding whatever phenomena occurred in the Fox home in Hydesville must be viewed with some suspicion. It will never be known what, if any, supernatural talents the Fox sisters may have possessed, but what is known beyond question is that, with a little aid, they were experts at self-promotion.

Under the careful tutelage of their elder sister, Leah, Margaret and Kate where taken to Rochester, New York, where they began to give "parlor seances" in some of the more affluent homes in the city. Here, the pair was able to reproduce the strange rapping that had first brought them to public consciousness and, still employing their alphabetical code, claimed to bring messages from the great beyond.

Soon hundreds were congregating at the seances, and the fame of the Fox sisters grew. So successful (and lucrative) were these events that eventually the older sister Leah, acting on "instructions from the spirits," rented a large downtown meeting hall in Rochester for her sisters to do a public presentation. This event was immediately sold out and more performances were scheduled.

Now the girls' fame truly began to catch hold. Newspaper articles concerning them appeared in several Rochester newspapers and then in newspapers in New York City. From there, the news spread to the press in Chicago and across the nation. Some of the articles hailed the pair as miracle workers, while others claimed to expose them as frauds. However, the controversy over their supposed powers only fed the fires of curiosity developing around them.

By now the Fox sisters had become big business, and soon Leah took her sisters on the road. As they began to play to larger and larger houses, their repertoire of "mediumistic skills" increased to include objects moving, tables rising and even, at one point, the spirit of Ben Franklin making an appearance to join in the fun.

As the storm of controversy continued to churn around them, their fame grew to even greater heights. No less a personage than P.T. Barnum brought the Fox sisters to New York City, where they "entertained" the likes of James Fenimore Cooper and Robert Ripley. Famed newspaper editor Horace Greeley gave the sisters living quarters in his mansion during the time they were in the city.

Following their popular run of public meetings in New York, the Fox sisters toured the country, playing to packed houses and choruses of both acclaim and disapproval from the press across the country. For the rest of their lives, they were never far from the limelight nor from controversy.

In their later years, tragedy and self-destruction followed closely at the heels of the sisters. Both suffered from lifelong struggles with alcoholism and frequent financial difficulties. In time, both were to die prematurely due to the effects of alcohol, financially destitute.

However, the final curious chapter in their lives was written several years prior to their deaths when Kate, perhaps seeking to regain the limelight once again, came forward in public to proclaim that she and her sister had been frauds.

To an astonished gathering in a hall in New York City, Kate announced that the pair had first produced the strange knockings in their farm house through the use of their big toes. Strange as the tale sounded, she assured the audience that she and her sister were each born with a big toe that cracked at the joint when flexed. When either placed her foot on a wooden board, as they had originally on the floor of their Hydesville home, and cracked the toe joint, the miraculous seemed to occur. The wood, acting as a sounding board, amplified the cracking sound and made it appear as though it was coming from another part of the room.

From the distance of many years, such a story seems almost as preposterous as some of the other tales that had been told by the girls, and no doubt some in the audience that night scoffed when hearing it. However, after explaining her method of producing the knocks, Kate then proceeded to take off her shoe and, placing her foot against the wooden stage, flexed the first toe of her right foot. Immediately the sound of knocking, which had so long ago launched the girls on their road to fame, echoed from the stage. The crowd went away convinced that night and it seemed as though spiritualism had been dealt a death blow.

However, as it has demonstrated throughout the years, spiritualism was not so easily vanquished. In the wake of the fame of the Fox sisters, countless other mediums had began to tour the country and indeed the world. Many produced the same sort of phenomena as had Margaret and Kate, but some stretched the bounds of mediumship further, adding new wonders and mysterious phenomena to their presentations.

Such mediums frequently toured the country going from city to city, selling out to large crowds of the curious and devout wherever they went. Millions became their followers, including some of the most affluent and famous people of their time. Mary Todd Lincoln is said to have had a special room in the White House reserved for her seances and later, the famed Sir Arthur Conan Doyle, creator of *Sherlock Holmes,* became an avid spokesman for spiritualism.

Of course spiritualism also has garnered its share of criticism as well. In particular it has found its greatest antagonists in the magical arts profession. Beginning with famed magician Harry Houdini, these illusionists, trained in the methods of duping an audience, have come forward to expose fraudulent mediums and the methods they have employed. In fact, many famous magicians have taken particular interest and pleasure in their persecution of spiritualist mediums.

However, despite the rancor of magicians and others, spiritualism has continued to survive through the years. In fact, in the late 1800s, so popular was spiritualism that traveling mediums began to quit their migratory ways to found permanent "spiritualist camps," to which the faithful would flock each summer. History reveals that by the early 1880s, no less than seventeen such camps had sprung up across the nation.

A combination of retreat center, summer camp and religious shrine, these camps did a huge business in the late nineteenth and early twentieth centuries. Participants were welcomed to come and camp on the grounds, or to rent rooms or cabins. The faithful would attend lectures given by prominent spiritualists of the day and nightly public or private seances put on by the host of resident mediums.

Perhaps the most well known camp in the nation and today the oldest, is located near Indianapolis in the small town of Chesterfield. Well renowned in spiritualist circles as a Mecca for supernatural activity, Camp Chesterfield was founded in 1887 and has been in continual use since that time. Growing from a few tents and ramshackle buildings, the camp has evolved into a sprawling campus of lodges and cottages, some to accommodate guests and some for the dozens of mediums who gather there each season. The first of several large meeting halls was built there in 1891, and since that time these halls have been used for large public seances as well as lectures.

Through the many years and despite countless efforts to discredit the activities housed there, Camp Chesterfield has survived. Some would credit this survival to the truth of the tenants taught there and others simply to the gullibility of the human spirit, but in the end, it must be said that those managing the camp have shown great resilience, as well as a good deal of ingenuity, in catering to the public thirst for the supernatural.

With the deep involvement of Camp Chesterfield in the realm of the "the spirits," it is only natural that a whole legion of ghost stories would evolve from the place. Ghosts have, after all, been the stock and trade of this camp for many years. However, the most unusual story to come from the camp is not one that is chronicled in the Chesterfield archives. In fact, the camp itself takes pains to deny that the incident occurred at all, yet the story has filtered down through the decades, primarily in the magical arts community of northwest Indiana. It is admittedly a rather bizarre ghost story, especially since it contains no ghost at all. In point of fact, this story is extraordinary because it is an *un*ghost story.

The tale begins in the late 1940's, when Camp Chesterfield and spiritualism in general were enjoying a renewed popularity in America. It has been well documented that, historically, spiritualism has prospered during and immediately after major wars, as those who lost family and friends to the conflict find themselves drawn to spiritualism in an effort to contact their dearly departed. Such was the case immediately after World War II, when hundreds from across the Midwest flocked to Camp Chesterfield, seeking the "manifestations" the mediums there were ready to produce— for a price.

As the summer session of 1949 began, a new medium rose as the shining star of Camp Chesterfield. Bearing the quaint title of "Madam Mimi,"* this particular medium soon became renowned among the spiritualist faithful for her full trance mediumship, including the channeling of unearthly voices as well as the production of "apports," or physical objects produced by the spirits.

Soon word of the seemingly extraordinary talents of this medium began to filter out into the surrounding communities and reached the ears of an Indianapolis newspaper editor named James Sevrin*. Sevrin, a veteran reporter and newspaper editor, viewed the tales of the ghostly phenomena produced by Madam Mimi with some skepticism, but thought them interesting enough to send a young reporter, Bob Leazenby,* down to the camp to attend one of her public seances. No doubt it was his intention for Leazenby to produce an exposé on the fraudulent practices employed by Madam Mimi and spiritualist mediums in general.

If this was indeed his intention, then the editor must have been gravely disappointed with the results. Within two days, the cub reporter was back in his office with an article relating, in glowing terms, the inexplicable phenomena produced by the medium. He had become a believer.

The meeting, he related, was held in one of the larger halls on the camp, with about a hundred people attendance. The evening began with about half an hour of singing, after which Madam Mimi, a short robust woman garbed in a flowing white robe, took the stage. Strolling to the podium in the center of the stage, Madam Mimi spoke for about twenty minutes, preaching of the truth of spirit communication and the wisdom imparted to her from her "spirit guides."

She then promised to provide proof of her spiritual powers. An assistant came on stage and draped a blindfold securely around the head of Madam Mimi. Next a bowl was produced containing small slips of paper. These slips, which had been distributed throughout the audience before the seance began, contained questions written by audience members. Madam Mimi emphasized that the questions had been kept backstage, unread by her or her assistants, until she called for them from the stage.

With great dramatic flair, Madam Mimi reached blindly into the bowl before her, retrieved one of the billets and held it to her forehead. Then, swaying slightly, Madam Mimi read out a question and gave a brief answer. A scream of delight from one of the audience members made it clear that she had correctly adduced both the question asked and the answer sought. Time and again Madam Mimi retrieved slips from the bowl before her, each time apparently reaching the right psychic vibrations with regard to the queries.

Next Madam Mimi removed her blindfold, left the stage and began to roam down one of the aisles of the hall. Stopping suddenly at the seat of one elderly man, she grasped his arm vigorously, closed her eyes and muttered, "The spirits tell me that you have lost someone near to you... a nephew perhaps?" Dumbly the man shook his head in assent. "Your nephew is here tonight," Madam Mimi intoned. "He says that his passing was difficult... was he killed in a forest?"

"Yes!" the elderly gentleman erupted, "in France!" "Your nephew wants you to know that he is at peace and his mother is here with him," Madam Mimi concluded.

"That's right—my sister died last year!" came the reply.

Now Madam Mimi continued up the aisle, stopping at the seat of a young woman. Once again, she grasped the woman's arm and pronounced that a elderly woman named Florence wished to convey her love to her and to say that she should make peace with her sister. At this, the young woman leapt up and hugged the medium, crying, "My mother... my mother!" before collapsing back into her chair in joyful tears.

Now came the climax to the evening. Madam Mimi once more climbed to the stage and the lights were dimmed. A large cabinet known as a "spirit cabinet" was wheeled out and opened for audience inspection. Several assistants came forward to tie Madam Mimi's hands securely behind her back. Next, Madam Mimi was placed on a small seat in the cabinet and her head tied with a band of cloth to a wooden post at the back of the cabinet.

Then the door to the cabinet was shut and the doors latched. One of the assistants then explained to those assembled that the spirit cabinet would allow Madam Mimi to "focus her spiritual energies" and that, since she was securely tied, any manifestations that might occur would clearly be the work of the spirits. He then retired from the stage, leaving the hall in silence.

In a few moments, however, the stillness was broken by the unearthly sound of a trumpet coming from within the cabinet. A strange tune echoed forth from the confines of the wooden box on stage and floated through the hall. This was followed a few moments later by the sound of a tom-tom being beaten repeatedly.

Immediately one of the assistants reappeared to open the cabinet, revealing Madam Mimi, her hands still tied behind her back and her eyes shut in what appeared to be a deep trance. Once again the door to the cabinet was closed, but this time a small aperture at the top of the door was opened, just above the level of the seated medium's head. With this, the assistant once more retired off stage and in a moment the most stunning phenomena of all became apparent.

Slowly at first and then faster, a white, vaporous substance appeared through the small opening. Increasing in volume, it billowed forth from the cabinet and stretched out toward the crowd. Someone in the front row audibly gasped, "My God, it's ectoplasm!"

Now from the midst of the white fog cascading from the top of the cabinet there appeared a spectral face. It was that of an Indian maiden, who peered out at the audience for a long moment before melting away, only to be replaced in a instant by the face of a young soldier. This face also disappeared behind the billowing mist and another face, that of a weathered old man with a long white beard, emerged.

For several paralyzing moments, this procession of faces continued and then, slowly, the white cloud emanating from the cabinet began to dissipate, some of it seeming to visibly withdraw backward into the box. An assistant came forward and opened the spirit cabinet. Madam Mimi, clearly exhausted form her ordeal, was untied and helped out.

The audience erupted into wild applause and the Bob Leazenby returned to his office in Indianapolis convinced that he had been present at a display of truly supernatural powers. By the time he stood before his editor's desk the next morning, his story in hand, he was a confirmed believer in spiritualism in general and most particularly in the powers of Madam Mimi.

After relating the events of that evening to his editor, the young reporter waited in expectant silence as Mr. Sevrin read the story he had written of it. When the wizened old editor finally looked up, his eyes seemed to twinkle with an odd mirth. "This is certainly an interesting story," the editor began, "and worth some investigation. However, before we print this story, I think we need to go back to see Madam Mimi. I even have a friend who might be interested in coming too." Unsure of just how to take this bit of news, Leazenby simply nodded his assent and added he was eager to go back at any time.

After the young man left his office that day, Sevrin thought for a moment and then, with a smile, picked up his phone and placed a call to an old friend in Hammond, Indiana. After hearing the story, the friend readily agreed to come down the next week with a friend to pay a visit to Madam Mimi.

Accordingly, the next week Sevrin accompanied Bob Leazenby to a restaurant a few miles from Camp Chesterfield. After a few moments, two gentlemen entered and made their way to the table. Sevrin rose and shook hands with the older of the two and then seated them. After coffee was served, introductions were made. The older gentleman, who sported a graying goatee beneath a hawk nose and dark eyes, introduced himself as Wayne Wirtz. His companion, a small, studious-looking young man, he introduced as Sam Nesbitt. The men, Mr. Sevrin explained, were "old friends who had an interest in spiritualism."

As the four sat and talked, Leazenby eagerly gave an account of what he had seen on his first trip to Camp Chesterfield. As he did so, he was somewhat puzzled to see his two new companions taking careful notes and sharing knowing glances at one another across the table. An hour later, the four found themselves seated in the large hall on the ground of Camp Chesterfield waiting for Madam Mimi to appear.

The seance that night was much the same as had occurred on the previous night, but was no less impressive to the young reporter. After the show had ended and the lights were brought up, Mr. Wirtz and Mr. Nesbitt spoke privately together for a moment and then suggested that the four meet again at the restaurant in about an hour. They then excused themselves, saying that they had "some business to attend to."

When the four met an hour later, the young Bob Leazenby was eager to hear if Madam Mimi had made believers of his three companions. Mr. Wirtz was the first to respond. "Oh, she made me a believer all right," he said with a chuckle. "I believe that she is a total fraud—and not a very good one, either."

"How can you be so sure?" gasped the reporter.

"Because," the older man responded, "we can do everything that she can—and better, too!"

At this point Sevrin interrupted. "Bob," he said, a wry smile crossing his face, "perhaps I should tell you a little more about my friends here." The pair, he revealed, were professional magicians, both members in good standing of the "Hammond Mystics," one of the oldest and most respected magician's clubs in Indiana. Furthermore, both were experts on the magic effects utilized by mediums to create their illusions.

James Sevrin explained to the young reporter that he had known Wayne Wirtz for many years since he had been a headline illusionist with the vaudeville circuit in Indianapolis. Mr. Nesbitt, he said, was a protégé of Mr. Wirtz and was known as a great historian of magic and magical effects. He had invited them, he said, to witness Madam Mimi's performance and give "another perspective" on the proceedings.

Patiently, Wirtz and Nesbitt then began to expound on the methods they believed the medium had used to sham the audience that night. Blindfolds, they explained, could readily be gimmicked to give the medium a clear view of questions written on paper slips. All the medium needed to do was to make her answers suitably vague and an impressive display of "psychic reading" was effected.

With regard to the impromptu psychic readings given members of the audience, Nesbitt explained that this too was an easy feat. He noted that it was common practice for mediums to put "plants" or cohorts in the audience prior to a seance to talk to audience members. With a few seemingly innocent questions, these allies were able to pick up information that, once relayed to the medium before she went on stage, would provide her with seemingly supernatural knowledge.

Finally, the two conjurers said that the "spirit cabinet" was simply an old magician's trick revisited. It was easy to appear to tie the hands of a person, in this case Madam Mimi, while in reality allowing them easy escape from their bonds. Once inside the cabinet, the medium could then produce endless apparitions with the aid of musical instruments and other paraphernalia hidden there. The so-called "ectoplasm" was nothing more than smoke and surgical gauze, unrolled so as to look, from a distance, like a flowing white vapor. A mask, hidden in the chamber and then produced behind such a fog would reveal a ghostly face of startling appearance.

With some difficulty, the pair were able to convince the young reporter that he had indeed been duped. Crestfallen and disillusioned, Leazenby remarked that now there was nothing to do but go back and write another story, this time revealing Madam Mimi as an utter fraud.

At this one of the magicians replied, "Not so fast young man—the fun is just beginning." The pair then related how, after the seance, they had gone back stage to meet with Madam Mimi's manager, posing as two "true believers in spiritualism." After extravagantly extolling the wonders of Madam Mimi, the pair inquired if it was possible to arrange for a private seance with the medium. After a satisfactory financial agreement was reached, a time was set for early the next evening, prior to the regularly scheduled public seance.

"Why do you want to go see her again?" inquired Sevrin. "You already know what she is doing—why get a second look?"

"Just be there tomorrow night at six," came the reply from Wayne

Wirtz, a mischievous grin crossing his face. "This is going to be fun."

The next evening, at the prescribed time, the four met outside the entrance to the hall and were ushered into a dark room backstage containing a large round table with heavy curtains cloaking each side of the room. In the center of the table sat a smoldering bronze brazier, sending rich scents into the room. A tall man in a dark suit informed them that they were very fortunate to receive a private seance from the renowned medium and that she would be present shortly.

In due course, Madam Mimi entered the room, resplendent in her flowing white gown, and greeted each man in turn. She then instructed the four men to sit with her at the table and to join hands in silence.

As the four men took their seats, the medium explained that she was about to go into a trance and that when the spirits manifested themselves, they were to remain absolutely still and silent. With these words, the medium lowered her head and shut her eyes in an attitude of rapt concentration.

After some moments, Madam Mimi began to roll her head back and forth, murmuring, "I feel the presence of spirits... are you here?" Suddenly a loud knock was heard emanating from the center of the table. Next, the sound of a spectral bell rang sweet and clear through the ambient air. In low tones, Madam Mimi adjured the spirits to make themselves known.

Abruptly, the table began to tip slightly on one end, as though lifted by a powerful hand, and then settled back to the floor. Again the sound of a bell filled the dark room. "The spirits are here!" Madam Mimi announced. Again, a loud knock sounded from the center of the table. "The spirits are strong this night," intoned Madam Mimi, her eyes still shut as though in a trance. "With whom do you wish to speak?"

She never received her answer. Abruptly, the table, which had tipped just moments before, lifted completely off the floor, levitating sideways in a long arc before landing back on the floor with a dull thud. Next an entire series of knocks erupted from the table until all present recognized the familiar cadence of "shave and a hair cut—two bits." Suddenly, the sound of a bell filled the room once again, this time ringing frantically. "Sounds like it's dinner time!" whispered the dark shape of Mr. Wirtz.

Suddenly, Madam Mimi's eyes snapped open and her head jerked forward. At that moment, the fire in the brazier erupted in a geyser of flames that shot three feet upward, sending sparks flying across the table.

It took a moment for the startled medium to regain her sight in the dark room. At first she could not believe what she saw before her. Through the darkness of the seance room, she could clearly see the figures of the four men seated before her, yet behind them she beheld a number of cadaverous faces peering down at her. Between them, in luminous letters across the dark air were the words, "Madam Mimi—FAKE!"

Suddenly the tones of an organ chord thundered through the room, followed in rapid succession by more loud knocking coming, it seemed, from the center of the table and the frantic clanging of the unseen bell. The table tipped once more and then was lifted at least a foot from the floor, despite the fact that those present still sat serenely in their seats, their hands joined on the elevated surface.

Perhaps a braver mystic might have stayed and attempted to recapture the situation. Madam Mimi, however, chose the better part of valor and opted for a quick escape. Standing up abruptly, Madam Mimi, in a voice choked with fear, uttered, "I don't know what the hell is going on here, but this ain't part of the act!" With this, she ran from the room. In a moment, the door was shut and the two magician present erupted in convulsive laughter.

Finding the light switch, Mr. Sevrin illuminated the room once more, revealing the papier-mâché masks and slate board painted with luminous letters that the magicians had used during the seance. "Well, boys, " Sevrin said with a smile, "I have to hand it to you. I knew you were up to something, but I had no idea what!"

"I'm just sorry the Madam left so soon" replied the younger magician, "We were just getting warmed up. The really good stuff was still coming!"

Madam Mimi did not appear for her public seance that night. According to the story as it has been told for many years, the esteemed medium packed her bags that evening and was never seen in Indiana again. The magicians packed their effects and returned to Hammond with another notch in their professional belts. Newspapermen Sevrin and Leazenby returned to Indianapolis to write their story, which ran on the front page the next week.

However, even today spiritualists continue to ply their trade across the country, offering hope for proof of an afterlife and providing, more often than not, the deceit of smoke and mirrors. Camp Chesterfield continues to thrive and vehemently disavows the presence of Madam Mimi on the campus, as well as the visit of magicians Wirtz and Nesbitt. While the camp does not deny the existence of fraudulent mediums, they still consider most mediums as genuine and staunchly defend the truth of the doctrines they promote.

However, if you ask a magician in Hammond about the subject, chances are he will ask you to sit for a while. Then, perhaps with a smug smile, he will tell you the greatest ghost story that never was.

7
A Historic Haunted Mansion
Madison, Indiana

Indiana is rich in tradition and history. From the industrialized regions of the north,west to the farms of central, Indiana to the sweeping hills and valleys that dot the southern Indiana countryside, our shared history is a part of the very texture of our state.

It is to Indiana's credit that much has been done to record and preserve this history. The Indiana Department of Natural Resources, Division of Museums and Historic Sites currently administers 17 historic homes and landmarks, which are open to the public. To tour one of these venerable structures is to take a walk through history. All have been carefully restored to their former grandeur, with attention to the smallest detail. Guides, acting as historical interpreters, lend their expertise in casting the unique spell of each of these dwellings, chronicling the past of both the home and its former inhabitants.

To amble through such a site truly does feel as though one is being drawn back through time. It is not surprising, then, that at least a few of these homes are said to be repositories of some distinctly odd revenants from their past. These are tales that do not usually appear on a tour itinerary.

One such site is the strikingly beautiful edifice known as the James F.D. Lanier Mansion, located in Madison, Indiana. Situated sedately next to the Ohio River, Madison is one of the most picturesque towns in the state. Known for the breathtaking beauty of its surroundings, Madison is also famous for the striking architecture that can be found throughout the town. Many homes dating back to the early nineteenth century have been painstakingly preserved, providing the town an atmosphere of gracious gentility.

Perched regally on a hillside overlooking the Ohio and the gray Kentucky mountains beyond, the Lanier Mansion has been called "a gem of Greek Revival architecture."[1] On the exterior, a spectacular two-storied portico overlooks the gardens to the front of the home. Inside, one is met with a sweeping spiral staircase, ornate carved cornices and moldings, and tall pine doors.

As impressive as the structure itself might be, the history of the mansion and the man responsible for its construction is even more interesting, for the legacy of James F. D. Lanier is an important part of the history of Indiana. His is the story of a courageous man who came to the aid of his state in the early days of its existence and changed the course of history.

James Lanier was born November 22, 1800, in Washington, North Carolina. It is ironic that this man who would come to play a major role in Indiana's efforts in the Civil War came from a proud southern lineage. As a young man, James Lanier moved with his family to Ohio where he received a primary education. In 1817, Lanier moved once again, this time to Madison, where his father ran a dry goods store and auction house

By age sixteen James showed a propensity for learning and after studying law with a local attorney, he went on to complete his education at the Transylvania School of Law in Lexington, Kentucky, graduating in 1823. After returning to Madison as prosecuting attorney, Lanier began to make his way up the professional ladder and in 1827, he was appointed clerk of the Indiana House of Representatives.

In 1833 Lanier shifted his efforts to banking, investing heavily in the newly formed Second State Bank of Indiana. In addition to serving as president of its Madison Branch and sitting on its board of directors, Lanier also became somewhat of a savior to the bank. When the economic panic of 1837 struck, the intrepid Lanier saved the bank from default by making a hazardous journey through hundreds of miles of wilderness to carry $80,000 in gold bullion to the U.S. Secretary of the Treasury in Washington, D.C. It would not be the last time his daring economic ventures would come to the aid of his state.

In 1840s Lanier, now married with seven children, decided to build a home worthy of his family and fortune. He purchased land along the Ohio River and commissioned architect and builder Francis Costigan to build a mansion at the exorbitant cost of $25,000. The mansion was completed in 1844 and the Lanier family moved into their stately new home.

As the years passed, Lanier's professional interests continued to grow. In time he became involved in the railroading industry, extending his financial empire by purchasing and selling railroad securities. However, his personal life suffered a shattering blow in April 1846 when his wife Elizabeth died of tuberculosis in their family home. Her funeral was held in one of the downstairs parlors. Two years later, James Lanier married Mary McClure, but once again ill fortune took a hand when their first child together died in infancy.

In 1851, perhaps saddened by the memories associated with the mansion, Lanier moved to New York City. However, he retained ownership of the home as well as his ties to Indiana. This turned out to be most fortunate, for soon the Hoosier state would be in urgent need of his help.

With the outbreak of the Civil War in 1861, Abraham Lincoln asked Governor Oliver P. Morton of Indiana to raise and equip a state militia of 6,000 men. Unfortunately, though plenty of able-bodied men were available for conscription, Governor Morton was confronted with a serious lack of armaments in the state. In fact, the entire arsenal of the state militia consisted of only 3,436 small arms and one six-pound cannon. In desperation, Morton turned to his old friend James Lanier. Within ten days of the attack on Fort Sumter, Lanier personally invested $420,000, a huge portion of his personal wealth, in state bonds. With these funds, the militia was outfitted and Indiana's part in the Union war effort was secured.

However, two years later, Indiana faced yet another economic crisis. As related in a history of the Lanier Mansion:

> As the winds of war fanned against the union, pro-confederate and pacifist elements in the state legislature blocked funds for the war effort and for the state debt payments. For a state that otherwise supported the Union, this was catastrophic. Governor Morton again appealed to Lanier, who now loaned $640,000 to pay two years of interest on the state's obligations. Without these funds, Indiana would have gone bankrupt. Moreover, Lanier did not expect to be repaid by a state in such financial straits."[2]

Once again, Lanier had come to the rescue of his beloved state. Though he would continue to live in New York until his death in 1881, he maintained a keen interest in the affairs of Indiana. As his son would later relate, "Despite the years and distance, my father always carried in his heart a great fondness for the Hoosier state."

After his permanent departure to New York, James F. Lanier left his Madison home in the care of his eldest son Alexander, formally deeding him the property in 1861 for one dollar. After Alexander's death in 1895, the mansion was in the possession of a series of relatives until Charles Lanier deeded it to the Jefferson County Historical Society in 1917. In 1925, the state of Indiana formally acquired the estate, which became Indiana's first official historic site.

Perhaps the most well-documented spirit said to linger in the Lanier Mansion is the famed "lady in red." Her first appearance is said to have been witnessed by a curator during the first year the old home was opened to the public. According to the tale, one afternoon shortly after closing hours, the woman was counting out money collected in the donation box on the first floor when she became aware of the feeling that she was being watched. Looking up, the guide saw a woman dressed in a Victorian-era red gown staring at her intently. Before the startled guide had a chance to react to this strange presence, however, the figure simply disappeared, seeming to evaporate into thin air. Thus was born the legend of the lady in red.

The most famous story of this lovely phantom, however, dates back to the spring of 1985. At the time historical interpreters, while present in the home, did not actually give guided tours of the mansion. Instead, when guests arrived to see the estate, it was the guides duty to meet them at the door, briefly tell the story of the home and then allow the guests to roam through the mansion at will. Frequently, after the guests had toured the second and third floors of the home, the volunteer would meet them at the bottom of the staircase and answer any questions about what they had seen.

According to the tale, one day a guide met a group of three older ladies who were coming down the staircase after finishing a tour of the mansion and asked them if they had any questions about the mansion. "No," came the reply from one woman in the group, "the woman upstairs explained everything beautifully." Somewhat puzzled, the guide asked the woman about whom she was referring to. "The woman in the antique red dress on the third floor. We did have some questions, but she answered them. She seemed to know all about the house," came her reply.

Puzzled, the guide knew that no other guide was on duty in the mansion that day and that no one else could have been present on the third floor. Later she mustered the nerve to climb the stairs to the third floor, only to find it empty.

Since that day, the story of the woman in the red dress has become quite well known in the community. However, verification of her presence is said to have come just a few years ago from an individual who had no prior knowledge of the tale. On October 19, 1996, a special event was going on at the mansion, complete with historical interpreters dressed in Victorian garb giving tours of both the mansion and the expansive gardens attached to it.

Among the tourists to walk through the home that day was a Hispanic woman who was vacationing in the area. After touring the home, she and her family moved into the gardens and were greeted by a gardener who asked them if they had enjoyed their tour of the building. After all agreed that they had, the middle-aged woman, in broken English, asked, "Do you have ghosts in the home?" Somewhat reluctantly, the volunteer admitted that there were stories of a ghost inhabiting the home and then asked why the woman was curious.

Now it was the visitor's turn to be abashed, but she haltingly explained that she had seen a foggy presence of a woman in her early thirties standing by the display case on the third floor. The woman, she added, was dressed in "*carmen*." Unsure of just what the woman meant, the gardener asked her to repeat herself. "The woman in carmen–she is a ghost. But don't worry–she seems friendly."

With a jolt of shock, the gardener realized two facts simultaneously. The first is that the word "carmen" is Spanish for "red." The second was that there was no guide dressed in red in the home that day. The lady in red had appeared again.

Interestingly, no one affiliated with the Lanier Mansion seems able to speculate as to the identity of the woman in red. It is known that the first wife of James Lanier, Elizabeth, died in the home, thus making her a possible suspect, but so rare are the appearances of this infamous phantom that no clear description of her has been ascertained. One thing that many associated with the home do believe, however, is that if the lady in red truly does lurk in the shadows of the Lanier Mansion, then she is in good ghostly company.

Many who have had inexplicable experiences in the mansion believe that there is not one, but several, ghosts in the home. Speaking with guides and workers in the home, it seems as if strange occurrences are commonplace there. While manifestations have been seen and heard throughout the home, it is said that the third floor, which once served as living quarters for servants and possibly for the children of the home, is particularly prone to mysterious happenings.

Deborah Moreland, who worked at the Lanier Mansion for four years, reports that staff, opening the mansion first thing in the morning, frequently find the blankets on the small bed on the third floor ruffled, as though someone had recently laid on them. This is doubly curious since the building is checked each evening before closing and remains empty and locked during the nighttime hours.

Other odd incidents seemed to center around the children's toys that used to be on display in the second floor bedroom, which had once belonged to Charles Lanier. In particular, one children's puzzle that laid on a table there showed a strange inclination for rearranging itself when no one was in the home.

"It was a puzzle of the United States," Ms. Moreland explains, "and we guides would have fun putting it together, yet often in the mornings we would walk in and it would be messed up, like a child had been playing with it."

Mike Linderman, former assistant curator at the home, also remembers a particular night when he discovered things amiss on the third floor.

"At the time, I lived across the street from the mansion," he recalls. "One of the strange things about the house was that the alarm had this annoying ability to go off at two or three o'clock in the morning. I usually would wait for the gardener to come deal with it, but one night she never came. The police had surrounded the house and so I went over.

"The Madison police are leery of the house themselves–they always made us go in first. When I went in, the alarm sensor said that the door between the east wing and the main house had been opened and closed, that there had been movement detected on the second floor. Yet, when we went in we found that the door between the wing and the main floor was still bolted shut. The cops and I searched the first and second floors but there was no one there. We were not up to going to the third floor that night, so we just reset the alarm and went home.

"However, when I came back the next morning I found that there were a lot of things rearranged on the third floor. Toys that had been on display up there had been moved around and one of the beds looked like someone had jumped up and down on it."

Other reports abound. Workers at the mansion have related the sound of phantom footsteps ascending the main staircase to the third floor. These footsteps have been heard by a great many staff members who have investigated the sounds only to find no human habitation on the floor. Interestingly, at least once the phantom footsteps elsewhere in the mansion may have inadvertently left a record of their passage. One longtime staff member vividly recalls the morning of March 19, 1996, when she and a colleague opened the home for the day and made a startling discovery. "We were on the second floor, where the wooden steps lead into a boy's bedroom. They had been sanding the floor and a thick coat of sawdust covered it. However, on the steps to the boy's room, there was a distinct set of small woman's footprints leading upstairs."

What made this discovery doubly perplexing was the fact that no footprints could be found in the sawdust in the hall leading to the stairs. They simply began at the base of the steps. "If someone had walked through the hall to those steps, we would have seen other footprints, but the only prints were on the stairs," the worker remembers.

Inexplicable sounds are said to have been heard from within the walls of the Lanier Mansion. The soft sound of children's laughter has been heard floating down from the third floor bedroom and on at least one occasion, the sound of a baby crying has echoed through the halls. As one worker recalls,:

In the winter of 1997 two male colleagues and I were on the third floor working on costumes and one of them had left the room to go downstairs. However, in a minute, he came back into the room and asked, "Did you *hear* that?" When we asked him what he meant, he told us that when he was in the hall, he had heard the sound of a baby crying coming from the north end. As he stood there wondering what a baby was doing up there, he heard the sound start coming toward him. It got louder as it got nearer and then the sound passed right by him and went into the south end of the hall. But he did not see anything.

Others have reported hearing the sound of furniture being moved in the upstairs bedrooms. However, when the rooms are checked all the furnishings are in their respective places. Bangs and thuds have frequently been heard coming from the area but when investigated nothing is out of place. Still others have reported the sounds of muffled voices coming from empty rooms.

In once such instance, Kate Branigin, the current curator at the mansion, was locking up for the night when she saw a light on in the third floor window. Reentering the house, she walked up the spiral staircase to the third floor, but as she reached the second floor landing, she was disturbed to hear the sound of at least two voices in muted conversation resonating down from the third floor. Knowing that she was alone in the house, the curator opted for the better part of valor and left the building rather than daring to venture to the third floor.

Another story of strange sounds emanating from the mansion centers around a tour guide who came to work at the mansion in 1997. His first encounter with whatever spirit lingers at the Lanier Mansion came shortly after beginning his work there. As the story is told, one day shortly after starting work, the guide was talking with several other staff members in the kitchen area of the house. The subject of ghosts was brought up and he scoffed at the stories of a spectral presence in the home. "If there is a ghost in this house," he said in a sarcastic tone, "let the kitchen door open now." His smile quickly faded, however, when, a moment later, the kitchen door opened, seemingly on its own power.

This was not to be the hapless guide's only encounter with the spirits of Lanier Mansion. During the first week of January in 1998, the young man appeared in the kitchen seemingly shaken and announced that he was taking a break from his work in the second floor office. When his fellow workers kidded him about taking a break after only a short time in the office, he stared at them and replied, "It is just too noisy up there." Realizing that there should be nothing to disturb the silence of the second floor, one of those present pressed him further. Finally the young man admitted that for the last three days that he had been working in the office, he had continually heard footsteps in the back hall between the two bedrooms. Repeatedly, he had gone to see who was there only to find he was apparently the only one present.

On hearing this report, his fellow worker counseled him to say the words, "In the name of Jesus, go away," whenever he heard the footsteps. Then, as though to emphasize her point, the worker turned her head toward the second floor landing and yelled, "Please be quiet, this man needs to complete his work!" Interestingly, the student later reported that after this conversation, he heard nothing more from the back hallway.

Yet more disconcerting were the sounds a furnace repairman recently heard while doing maintenance work in the building. According to a staff member, the repairman came in one morning and went to work in the basement. Shortly after arriving, however, the man reappeared in the kitchen and announced to workers there that he was taking an early lunch and would return later. Something in his demeanor must have alerted the staff members, one of whom questioned him as to the reason for his early departure. Reluctantly, the man admitted that, while working in the basement, he had repeatedly heard the sound of breathing and moaning close to his ear. "He left pretty quickly after that," the staff member recalls.

Guides also report that many guests at the home choose not to enter the third floor bedchamber, sensing a strange feeling about the room. "It seems that many people just feel a discomfort with the third floor," comments one longtime worker.

However, the third floor bedroom is by no means the only location in the Lanier Mansion where inexplicable phenomena seem to occur. Footsteps, voices and strange sightings have been reported throughout the home. Many of the longtime workers at the site tell stories of odd occurrences there.

One such worker is Cookie Block, a gardener at the estate. "I personally have never seen anything but I have heard plenty," she reports with a chuckle. "It happens to me usually in the mornings because I am the first one here.

"I have come in and heard people walking. There have been a few times when I have heard someone walking back to the mansion from the east wing on the main floor. I was in the south parlor one day, checking some flower vases ,and I distinctly heard someone walk up behind me.

This was before we had carpeting, so I could clearly hear their steps. I thought it was one of the other workers but when I turned around, there was no one there. I had hair standing up on the back of my neck on that one. That was the worst I have been scared here. Sometimes, when I hear them, I will just yell out, 'OK, that's it, I'm here, now go to bed!' and it will usually stop."

On another recent occasion, it was not footsteps but dancing that Cookie heard echoing through the mansion. "In December of 1997, I was in the south parlor, placing some ornaments on our Christmas tree. I remember it was about seven A.M. and I was up on a seven-foot ladder replacing some ornaments. I had Christmas music on, but over the music I suddenly heard what sounded like dancing on the floor upstairs. That, of course, was odd, but what was weirder yet about this was the fact that the dancing was heard on bare floors and the floor above is carpeted."

What gives credence to this story is the fact that the phantom footsteps were also heard by two other workers the same morning. Shortly after Cookie had heard the strange sounds, two other workers came into the north parlor and heard the same noises emanating from the floor above them. Both say they remember the incident clearly today.

Another strange episode reported by Cookie also took place in December, this time in 1998. "I was in the north parlor plugging in the Christmas tree when I heard a clinking sound. I listened and it sounded like the glass prisms on a lamp on the second floor being jiggled. Then I heard a man's stern voice say, 'Quit that!' and suddenly the clinking sound stopped. It was as clear as day, like a father telling a child to stop playing with the lamp. I went to the bottom of the staircase and looked upstairs, but there was nothing–no sound and no one there."

Like Mike Linderman, Ms. Block has been the victim of the strange malfunction of the alarm system in the mansion. She reports that since she lives close to the estate, she has frequently been called upon to respond to late night alarms in the building. "When I get here late at night, the inside doors have sometimes been found open," she says. "That should not happen–there are locks and bolts on most of the doors and there is no way that air could do that–there is no moving air in this house. Some nights I have been called in because motion had been detected on the third floor but when we go up there, there's never anything up there."

Mike Linderman also reports being witness to peculiar events. "One day," he remembers, "I was upstairs in the third floor office. I was up there by myself and the only other person in the house was another employee who was downstairs. Suddenly I distinctly heard footsteps coming up the stairs. You could clearly hear the footfalls coming up the staircase, all the way up to the third floor. I thought that it was the other employee, but just then I happened to pick up the phone and heard her voice from the phone downstairs. She had heard the steps too and all of a sudden we both realized that we knew where the other person was. Each of us had thought it was the other person on the stairs. It was just a bit spooky..."

Interestingly, both Cookie and Mike have come to the conclusion that most of the manifestations occur in conjunction with some sort of change or turbulence in the mansion. Cookie notes that during those times when renovation was occurring in the home or when there was discontent among the workers, the phenomena become more noticeable and intense.

This feeling is shared among a number of staff people, including Deborah Moreland, a former worker. Moreland seems to have encountered the strange goings on at the Lanier Mansion with some regularity during her four year tenure there. "The most common thing, I guess, is the footsteps," she reflects. "Over the past few years, I have heard them maybe a dozen times. They are very distinct footsteps." Interestingly, she does not seem to be disconcerted by the sounds echoing through the house. "You just kind of get used to it," she says. "After a while you don't notice them anymore. It blends in with the house noises. It does not bother me anymore–I live with it."

A bit harder to ignore are some of the other experiences Moreland has had. "Once, early in the morning, Cookie and I were the only ones around–no one was due in for several hours," she recalls. "Cookie was in the garage and I was alone in the house. I was upstairs in the office area and I was emptying trash cans and I heard the sound of someone trying to get through the door, like they were trying to work the mechanism of a doorknob. It was the door from the main house to the wing–it was bolted and someone was trying to get through. I yelled out 'Cookie,' because I thought it was her, but as it turned out there was no one in the house. I came down and searched the house but there was no one there at all.

"I have also walked into the library and smelled the odor of a fire from the fireplace, like the embers had just gone out. And of course, we never have fires in that room. Sometimes I have smelled the smell of pipe tobacco very distinctly in the library. It was really strong–I grew up with the smell of pipe tobacco and I recognize it. But of course, there is no smoking in the mansion."

Not only did Deborah hear and smell strange things in the mansion, but she has also seen some unexplainable things as well. "The first thing I ever actually saw," she says, "was a shadow. I was just finishing giving a tour and I was walking down from the third floor with a group of people about ten feet behind me. As I walked down the stairway, I saw that there was a shadow in the hallway. It was such that it had to be created by someone in the hallway or from the little room next to the bed chamber. It definitely was created by something solid- it was blocking light, but it seemed to be wavering slightly. I stepped forward to see what was causing it and suddenly it was gone. When I got to where it had been, there was nothing there."

This would not be Moreland's last strange sighting. In early January, 1999, she was to catch her first fleeting glimpse of whatever it is that inhabits the house. As she tells the story:

> It was early in the morning and a coworker and I were on a ladder in the south parlor taking down Christmas decorations. I had just gotten up on the ladder when I happened to look to the side and saw someone walking past the door from the house. I hollered at whoever it was, thinking it was one of the other workers, but no one answered. Then I got off the ladder, went through the library and into the back hall but there was no one there. What I had seen was definitely not a worker in the house. I only had time to see a quick glanc it was a figure of a person wearing a tan colored outfit. I only got a fast glance but it was definitely a person.

Interestingly, on other occasions staff members have reported glimpsing a woman clad in a tan colored outfit in both the cook's room and in the first floor hallway.

Another series of sightings has centered around the second floor master bedroom. One staff person, walking by the open door to the room, was amazed to glance through the doorway and see a woman in black sitting on the bed, rolling what appeared to be bandages. Workers and volunteers in the mansion also have reported seeing a man in a dark suit standing alone in the room one afternoon. There were no workers on duty matching either description.

Kate Branigin, the current curator of the Lanier State Historic Site, has also reported a number of seemingly inexplicable experiences there. "Once, in the summer of 1998, I was in the great hall on the first floor with Cookie when we heard women's voices coming from the gift shop area. It was a Monday, and the house was closed to the public, so we went to investigate. When we got to the gift shop, which was a short walk through the back hall, there was no one there. The curator at the time was upstairs and we went to him and asked if his wife, the gift shop manager, was in the house, or if he had waited on anyone in the gift shop, and he said 'no.' What was really strange was that both Cookie and I heard voices in the shop, but the curator, who was actually closer, heard nothing."

Branigin relates several other odd experiences at the mansion, including one that occurred on a damp, dark evening in November of 1998. As she tells the tale, "Shortly after I was promoted to curator, I was the last one to leave one evening As I exited the house I looked back and realized that the third floor lights had been left on. I re-entered the house with the intention going to the third floor to turn off the lights.

"Normally, I will enter the house and 'greet' the ghosts if I am alone, so they will know I am coming (even though I credit myself as a nonbeliever), but this night I didn't. As I reached the second floor landing, I heard hushed voices coming from the third floor. I turned around and left immediately."

Many other workers and visitors to the mansion report seeing and hearing unusual things in the building. Perhaps the most dramatic sighting in the house, however, deals with a civil war reenactor who visited the home several years ago. Each autumn for many year, the staff hosted "River Days," a weekend-long series of events designed to celebrate the mansion and its history. Guides dressed in nineteenth-century garb gave tours of the home and a variety of special activities were held.

For several years, as a part of this event, a troupe of Civil War reenactors were invited to come in costume and visit the grounds in honor of Mr. Lanier's role in the Union war effort. According to a meticulous journal of events at the Lanier Mansion kept by a longtime staff person, a rather disquieting episode occurred during the reenactment that was held on August 16, 1986. At the time, the curator of the mansion lived in the east wing of the mansion. As a courtesy to the Civil War reenactors present that day, the curator offered the use of her bathroom and shower so as to allow them some vestige of modern convenience.

Late that afternoon, one of the "soldiers" was making his way from the camp setup (in what is now the garden area of the yard) to the house to use the facilities. As he did so, he happened to glance up at a second floor bedroom window and saw the face of a man staring down at him intently. Thinking that this was one of the historical interpreters taking a break from a tour, the reenactor thought no more about this figure until late that evening, when this face and presence was brought back to him in a very dramatic and some might say, shocking way.

That night, the curator generously invited some of the reenactors to her apartment in the east wing of the home for coffee and conversation. During the course of the evening, she began to tell her guests about the history of the home and went to a bookshelf to bring down a box of photos she had assembled of Lanier family members. As she went through the photos of family members, giving a brief history of each, she happened to bring out one particular photo that elicited a strange reaction from one of the men present.

Before she could begin to expound upon the history of this particular family member, the curator notice that the man in question had turned white and was shaking visibly. When she asked him if he was feeling well, the man exclaimed in a low, nervous voice, "I saw that man this afternoon!" When questioned as to the meaning of his strange statement, he excitedly told of seeing the face at the window staring down at him. Apparently shaken from his experience, the man then excused himself from the gathering and went back to the safety of his encampment in the yard. Later the next day, the man spoke to several workers and confirmed what he had clearly seen.

While such a dramatic scenario would seem extraordinary at any other location, at the Lanier Mansion it may be deemed almost commonplace. In a review of the vast collection of inexplicable events recorded there, an entire catalogue of seemingly supernatural manifestations emerges. From the fated lady in red to the myriad of other spirits seen, heard and felt within these antique walls, in this beautiful historic mansion, it seems that phantoms walk the halls and restless spirits linger in the shadows.

8
The World's Largest Ghost Hunt
Porter County, Indiana

Her presence has been described as mysterious and sad, yet oddly alluring. The factual basis of the tale told of her is still debated by many local historians. Yet the power of her legend still remains. It is a power that still reaches out today and a power that not so long ago resulted in the largest recorded ghost hunt in history

This is a story that begins with the sad tale of a woman lost to a cruel fate and ends in a very modern tale of what some have described as "acute mass hysteria." The legend of the "Lady in White," as she has come to be known, begins in the latter decades of the nineteenth century. Although many different variations of the tale have been told, one of the most common stories begins when a train arrived in Porter County, Indiana, from Chicago. As the steam locomotive ground its way to a slow stop, a tall, willowy young woman disembarked, carrying a large cloth covered bag. Exuding a quiet air of East Coast aristocracy, the statuesque woman was a striking figure with her long dark hair flowing down past her slender neck, cascading ringlets on the shoulders of her green silk dress.

Her name, some say, was Annabel and she came from a proper Boston family. Bright and vivacious, Annabel had graduated from a private school at age sixteen. At the time her family thought that she would enter East Coast society. However, much to the disapproval of her parents, Annabel had felt the call of adventure and announced that she had been accepted for a position as a schoolteacher in the rugged farmland of northern Indiana. Shortly thereafter, she boarded a train bound for Chicago and a few days later, Annabel stepped into the bright sun of a beautiful Porter County day.

Soon Annabel was settled into her one-room schoolhouse that would be her world for the next period of her life. Though initially viewed with some suspicion as "an Easterner," Annabel soon won the acceptance and respect of many of the farm families by her kind ministrations to their children and her undying dedication to bringing education to those entrusted to her care. Annabel spent her days tirelessly teaching the young and maintaining the schoolhouse. In the evenings, as was the custom at the time, she took her lodging in the homes of her students.

Annabel found her job exhausting yet fulfilling. She threw herself completely into her work and in return, she was gratified to see her students blossom in the gentle light of education. Still, at odd moments, the girl allowed herself to ruminate about her former life, and at such times she felt a keen sense of loneliness for her family and for the company of those her own age.

As her first long, dreary Indiana winter finally warmed to glorious spring, the loneliness began to abate as Miss Annabel began to "keep company" with a young farmhand in the region. His name was Matthew and he was known in the region as an honest, hard-working young man with a good future. At age twenty, three years Annabel's senior, he was also tall and ruggedly handsome.

His attentions to Annabel began subtly enough. They had met at a social event at a local church and before long, his horse-drawn buggy was seen taking Annabel to and from her duties at the schoolhouse. Local tongues wagged, but the young couple, oblivious to all but each other, continued to enjoy their time together. In time, fondness turned to true love and a wedding was planned. A golden, peaceful future stretched out before them as they sat on the Lake Michigan shoreline and dreamed of a home and family together.

In August, just before the school year was to begin, Annabel married her handsome lover in a simple church service. Her family in Boston, horrified at the path chosen by their daughter, was not present.

The pair moved into a small home in northern Porter County where

Annabel could continue to teach and her husband could begin to farm for himself. However, farming in this area proved difficult at best. Since the young couple did not have the financial means to purchase land in the fertile farmland just a few miles south, they made do with somewhat marshy, sandy soil to plant their crops. It was a hard, poverty-ridden existence, yet the pair seemed happy together. All in all, despite their sometimes dire financial straits, the newlyweds seemed well on their way to the happy future they had envisioned for themselves.

When, a year later, their first child, a son, was born, Annabel quit teaching at the one room schoolhouse. With the loss of her income as a teacher and with three mouths to feed, Matthew found himself working night and day to provide for his family. In time, the stress placed upon him began to tell and Matthew began to take solace in a bottle. Annabel found that her husband would return form his labors silent and grim, only to drink himself into a stupor before the fire each night.

As his drinking continued, Matthew's character began to change as well. Formerly attentive and loving, the once gentle farmer turned cold and mean to his family. According to legends told, his temper would often flare when drunk and he would lash out at his hapless wife and child.

Finally, one cold night after a particularly brutal beating, Annabel knew that she could stand this life no longer. Waiting till her husband had passed out in his rocking chair, the young wife packed a few belongings, gently took her son from his cradle and made her way out of the house forever. As she paused by the door to the small home she looked back once more and felt hot tears stream down her cheeks. In her there rose a feeling of mourning for the husband she had lost and the dreams that would never come to be. In a poignant and sad farewell, she went back and silently kissed Matthew on the cheek. Then Annabel and her son were out into the cold night air.

It was her intention that night to make her way to the home of a friend who lived just a mile away. She hoped to persuade the woman to allow the pair to stay in their home for a few days, till she could find a way to get back to Boston and throw herself at the mercy of her family. She would never make it that far.

As she walked through the fields that night, she felt the stiff cold from the frozen earth work itself up through her shoes and into her thin stockings, but she dared not slacken her pace. The full moon, which she had counted on to help guide her through the woods, was obscured behind a thick veil of white as a sudden snow squall erupted around her. Stumbling along in the world of white that had suddenly enveloped her, her child held close to her shoulder, Annabel lost her way. Realizing her predicament, the young woman began to search frantically for some landmark she could recognize, in the process making her way deeper and deeper into the woods. As she did so, she felt the numbing cold creep up her body, yet still she fought for her life and the life of her child.

Some three days later, after the blizzard had abated and a search conducted, the bodies of Annabel and her son were found stiffly frozen in a snow bank. Matthew tried to pacify his neighbors with the story that his wife had simply gone out on an errand and gotten lost, but few believed him. In the end, the two were laid to rest in a small plot of earth next to the farm they had died trying to escape.

Yet, it is said, the spirit of Annabel has not lain quiet. For, on certain nights when the moon is full, those passing by what is now Campbell Road in unincorporated Porter County have claimed to have seen the figure of a woman in white, beckoning to them from a grove of trees. Over the ensuing decades, many have claimed to see her and some say that it is the spirit of Annabel, still trying to escape the purgatory that her life and death have become. It should be clearly noted that many legends have sprung up explaining this presence and the story of Annabel cannot be verified by any historical records, yet all of the variant tales agree on one point: the woman is young and seems to be seeking help from those to whom she appears.

In the end, nothing will truly be known about who this woman might be or what eternal aid she is seeking, but one thing is quite certain: this story has been passed down from generation to generation in Porter County and many, particularly the young, have actually gone out in search of the phantom of Campbell Road.

It was just such a search that resulted in an event that later would draw international attention. It began innocently enough in late October 1965 when several local teenagers began to tell their friends of a strange and enigmatic encounter with the phantom of the Lady in White. According to the report, four of the teenagers were driving along Campbell Road when suddenly the driver, glancing into the darkness, was shocked to see the form of a woman in a long white dress standing forlornly a few hundred feet from the roadside.

Swerving his car to the side of the road, the driver and his occupants emerged to see the figure gesture toward them and then disappear into the marshy woods. As the teenagers ran after the woman, an eerie cry floated out to them through the evening stillness. It was the mournful cry of a woman pleading, "Help me!" According to the reports, the teenagers ran into the woods, but the woman in white was gone.

Such reports are the general stuff of American folklore and might have simply been relegated to such status had not the story begun to circulate widely in the surrounding areas. Young people, hearing the story from their classmates, repeated it to their parents, who in turn remembered other stories of such sightings. Before long, the entire community of Chesterton and Porter, as well as the outlying areas, were buzzing with the stories of the Lady in White. New reports surfaced daily and old stories were rehashed and enlarged with each retelling. With Halloween approaching, the fame of the Lady in White was reborn.

As October wore on, at first a few and then a steady stream of cars could be seen patrolling Campbell Road, looking for an appearance of the famed lady. Soon the stream turned to a flood, as at first hundreds and then thousands of people came to the area with the hope of seeing, or even "laying" the ghost. A carnival-like atmosphere began to prevail, with cars parked along both sides of the road and searchers, both teenagers and adults, combed the woods for some sign of the specter.

Some came forfeited with "liquid courage" (spirits to help one confront a spirit) and still others brought shotguns determined to shoot the ghost if it appeared. Only luck prevented this dangerous combination from producing yet another tragic story linked to the area.

As the number of searchers increased each night, neighbors began to complain. Several reported their land invaded, their fences damaged and their sleep disturbed by the sound of shotguns being fired into the air. The Porter County sheriff's office sent officers to the area but even they were unable to contend with the volume of people. By the first week of November, with crowds estimated as high as six thousand people coming to the area, the state police were brought in. The area was cordoned off and several arrests were made. As one state police officer was quoted as saying in a local paper, "It is like a zoo out here. We have a few thousand people, a few armed drunks, and they are all here to see a ghost."

Interestingly enough, the one person who did not see fit to attend the festivities was the Lady in White. Whether shy by nature or just unwilling to brave the onslaught of the curious, no sightings of her were reported during the last week of October or the first week of November.

Needless to say, such a story could not escape the attention of the local and state media. Stories about the ghost hunt were carried by all of the national wire services and the story was picked up nationally and even internationally.

Though the mass hysteria faded quickly in the Chesterton area as teenagers and adults gave up ghost hunting to get back to the business of living, the story continued in other circles. Such was the case of a film crew from the British Broadcasting system who came to Chesterton in 1978 to film a documentary on the ghost hunt. The crew stayed for a week in the area, interviewing local residents and former ghost hunters. The title given the segment was, "The World's Largest Ghost Hunt."

Today, the area of Campbell Road where once the ghost was said to walk is quiet and serene again. Occasionally, a carload of curiosity seekers will slow down on a moonlit night in an effort to catch a glimpse of the Lady in White, but by and large the story has been forgotten. This is exactly as local residents would like to have it. As one longtime neighbor puts it, "I was here for all that hysteria and I'm glad that it's over. I have lived here for many years and I never have seen the ghost, but, by God, those ghost hunters were a scary bunch."

9
Two Troublesome Hoosier Poltergiests
Kokomo, Indiana &
Odon, Indiana

Of all the varied species of the undead, perhaps the most mysterious and bizarre is the poltergeist. Taken from the German (meaning "noisy ghost"), the term poltergeist and the strange phenomena they are said to wreak have been reported for centuries from all over the world. The renowned nineteenth-century investigator of psychic phenomena, Harry Price, in his exhaustive study, *"Ghosts Over England,"* described a poltergeist as:

> ...an alleged ghost, elemental or "familiar," with certain unpleasant characteristics. Whereas the ordinary ghost is a quiet, inoffensive and rather benevolent spirit, the poltergeist is just the reverse. According to many reports...the poltergeist is mischievous, destructive, noisy, cruel, erratic, malicious and ill disposed.

With such an unflattering reputation, it is understandable that a poltergeist might well be (in the words of the venerable Dr. Price) "ill-disposed." In fact, however, this characterization does seem to fit. Poltergeist phenomena usually include strange noises, the seemingly inexplicable movement of objects (often in plain sight of many witnesses), foul odors, and objects spontaneously catching fire. Those present at the time of such outbreaks often report the sensations of being shoved, slapped or choked by unseen hands. In one rather spectacular and legendary case known as the "Bell Witch of Tennessee," a poltergeist was even blamed for poisoning a man.

As incredible as such a description of events might sound, in truth poltergeists are among the most commonly reported hauntings and certainly have been among the most carefully studied. Indeed, poltergeist phenomena lends itself well to such study, since the phenomena tends to occur at all hours of the day and night, often in front of seemingly reliable witnesses.

It is just such research study that has led many twentieth century investigators to speculate that perhaps poltergeist phenomena might not be the activity of a ghost at all, but instead might be the unwitting result of a living agency, particularly an adolescent child. This theory stems from the fact that nearly all poltergeist activity as it has been reported does not seem to be linked to a geographic location, but rather to a person. Most often, this person is an adolescent, particularly a young girl. These unlucky young people seem to be the focal point of the activity and often receive the brunt of the phenomena's destructive power. Researchers have long noted that in nearly all cases of poltergeist activity, an adolescent was present in the home, and in some cases when the young person was removed from the home, the activity vanished or even followed the young person to the new location.

While some point to this fact as an indication of fraud on the part of the young person, others suggest that perhaps the phenomena is somehow related to his or her emotional state. Perhaps, as some have theorized, emotional or psychic trauma, common in adolescents, might in odd cases release a hidden and unknown power of the mind resulting in what the researcher J.B. Rhine called "spontaneous psychokinetic disturbances." This is to say that perhaps the entire realm of what is known as poltergeist activity may be the psychic lashing out of a mind driven to distraction by emotional stress.

Such theories are, of course, speculative at best. In the realm of parapsychological studies, the nature and even existence of poltergeist activity is still hotly debated. What cannot be denied, however, is that poltergeist phenomena have been reported for centuries from all over the world and such reports continue to filter in today. With the widespread nature of such reports, it is not surprising then, that the Hoosier state would be unable to escape the ravages of such "ill-disposed spirits."

Such is the case of John and Mary Spurning,* who live on a quiet residential street just outside of Kokomo. To see the sedate two story home sitting serenely on the tree-lined avenue, it is hard to imagine that briefly the home was the site of events that stretch the limits of understanding and destroyed the peace of their loving family for several weeks in 1977.

John, a quiet, bespectacled executive with a local electronics firm, speaks of the incidents reluctantly. "It all seems like a dream now," he says with the hint of a sigh, "a bad dream. I guess I have tried to block it out from my memory in recent years. But you cannot forget entirely." Mary, his wife of thirty-five years, views the events with a bit more interest. "It was an unforgettable time all right," she now says. "It was unbelievable, really. But even at the time, it had a kind of excitement to it, too."

The events in question began in June 1977, when the Spurnings opened their home to their sixteen-year-old niece Brenda. "Brenda's father, who is John's brother, took a job that required the family to move overseas for a year," Mary recalls. "But Brenda did not want to go. She was going to be in her senior year of high school and she really wanted to finish up school in Kokomo, so John and I said that she could live with us for a year. Our daughter Amy, who was eight at the time, was excited about having a big sister for a year, and since Brenda was such a quiet, well-mannered girl, we knew she would be no trouble."

As Mary and John would soon learn, however, sometimes "trouble" follows even quiet, well-mannered children. In this case, the trouble would be of a strange and inexplicable nature.

"The first thing that I remember happening," John recalls, "was a noise. It was in early June, about a month after Brenda had come to live with us. It was about 9:00 at night and Brenda and I were in the living room when suddenly I became aware of a tapping noise in the wall. At first it was just a light ticking sound and then it got louder. It seemed to be coming from the wall behind the couch where Brenda was sitting. I was reading my paper at the time but after a few minutes, when the tapping persisted, I looked over at Brenda and said, 'Are you doing that?' but she just looked at me wide-eyed and said no."

Rising to investigate, John found that the sound was indeed emanating from the wall just a few feet from where Brenda was sitting. Thinking that a mouse had somehow gotten into the wall, John made mental note to set some traps the next day, but just then the strange tapping suddenly shifted to a wall on the opposite side of the room. "I thought, 'My God this is odd,' John now says, "and I walked over to the other wall to listen to this tapping but when I got there, suddenly the tapping turned to this thunderous pounding. It was like someone was slamming their first into the wall again and again."

At about this time Mary, who had been upstairs with their young daughter, came running down to see what all the commotion was about. "I had heard the noise and wondered what could possibly be going on down there. It sounded like John was tearing the place apart and so I ran downstairs to find out what was going on. When I got there, I found John standing next to the wall just staring and Brenda on the couch curled up, looking frightened," Mary says.

After John explained the situation to his startled wife, the two tried to decide what they should do. Mary suggested that the culprit could be water pipes banging as they sometimes do when air gets into the system, but John explained that no water pipes ran through that particular wall of the home. "We talked about it for about five minutes, trying to figure out what to do," Mary says. "The whole time we talked this hammering just got louder and louder. Then suddenly it just stopped. It was like someone had turned off a switch."

Unable to come up with any adequate explanation for what had occurred, John suggested that they call a contractor the next day to look at the structural integrity of the wall. Mary then herded her family off to bed, hoping that the events of that night were simply an odd, singular occurrence. The next week was a quiet one in the Spurning home and John put off his promise to call the contractor.

The odd noise was fast fading into memory three weeks later when suddenly, it was brought to mind once more by another strange occurrence. "It was about 10:30 on a hot July night," John remembers. "I remember because we had all of the windows open and I still could not sleep owing to the heat. Suddenly I heard a noise like an explosion from the basement, where Brenda had her bedroom. It literally shook the house—I thought for a minute that a truck had somehow run off the street and hit the house or that maybe the gas furnace had exploded. Then I thought of Brenda and came flying downstairs as fast as I could."

Running into the basement room that had been converted into a bedroom for his niece, John found the girl sitting up with a terrified expression on her young face. "She was badly frightened," Johns says, "and I asked her what had happened. She said she had no idea–that she had been sleeping when suddenly she heard this noise. She had been too scared to get out of bed." Strangely, as John looked around the basement, he could find no evidence of an explosion or impact of any kind. The gas furnace remained was turned off and had been since that spring, and none of the furnishings seemed to have been disturbed.

"I was shocked, of course," says Mary, "but while John investigated the rest of the basement I just tried to calm Brenda down. Then after a few minutes, John came back and said that everything was all right and we should all go to bed. I could tell from his expression he was upset but I did not want to question him in front of our niece, so I just kissed Brenda goodnight and went up to bed."

John and Mary climbed back into their bed and began a whispered conversation about the strange incident. Just then their peace was shattered by another sound coming from the basement. This time it was the unmistakable sound of breaking glass.

Once again running for the basement stairs, John flew down but by then the sound had stopped as quickly as it had begun. "I went to Brenda's room and this time she was lying in bed with the covers over her head. I could tell she was sobbing. I asked her if something had broken and she said she did not know what was going on, but it had come from the pantry next to her bedroom. I told Mary, who had followed me down, to stay with Brenda and I walked into the pantry. It was a mess."

John continues, "Mary had jars that she stored on the shelf for canning and about half of them were on the floor in pieces. At first I thought a shelf had broken but I could see the shelves were just fine. I also noticed that some of the jars were all the way across the room, like they had been thrown from the shelves hard. I could not believe it. I hate to admit it but at that moment I thought Brenda was doing this–that she was causing all the strange things going-on."

Such a suspicion, while natural, was short lived. "I stood there in the pantry looking at the mess," John says, "and Mary came to the door behind me. I heard her choke back a scream–those were, after all, her canning jars. She said, 'John, what is going on here?' and I was about to answer when suddenly one of the empty jars on the shelf across the room just exploded."

"It was like a stick of dynamite had gone off in that jar. Shards of glass went flying and one stuck me on the face just below my left eye. Then, almost before I could move, two other jars next to the first one exploded as well. I grabbed Mary and said, 'Let's get the hell out of here.' "

With Brenda in tow, the pair went upstairs. Amy, their young daughter, was taken from her bed to sleep with her mother and father, while Brenda simply curled up on a blanket at the foot of John and Mary's bed. Clearly, the entire family was badly shaken and all three wondered aloud what could be causing these bizarre happenings. In the end, they eventually drifted off to sleep.

When the daylight came, John called his office and said he would be taking the morning off. Over breakfast, all four members of the family spoke of the weird events of the night before. Mary wondered if the house could be haunted, but John dismissed this idea immediately. He did not believe in ghosts and besides, they had lived in the home for ten years without any similar incidents. While they did not discuss it, neither John nor Mary was willing to discount the possibility that Brenda was somehow behind the strange occurrences, yet logic argued against this assumption too. Neither her nature nor previous behavior suggested a destructive bent in the girl and besides, how could the girl have made an empty jar explode on a shelf while she cowered in the next room?

In the end, John concluded that some strange natural force must be at work. Perhaps earth tremors were causing the basement walls to shake. Perhaps the home's foundation was shifting, causing the disturbances. In any case, he surmised, it was time to make good on his promise to bring in a professional contractor. Going to the phone, John placed a call to neighbor who, he knew, worked both as a building contractor and as an inspector for the city. After vaguely explaining that the house was "doing strange things," John elicited a promise from the man to meet him at the home that afternoon at five in the afternoon.

True to his promise, the contractor arrived at the home that afternoon and, along with John, gave the building a thorough inspection. Nothing out of place could be found. While the foundation had indeed shifted over the fifty-year history of the house, no stress was being placed on basement walls. The electrical system was up to date and the plumbing seemed in good working order. Altogether the house seemed to be structurally safe and sound with no apparent cause for the disturbances that had occurred. Concluding that he had nothing to report to the Spurnings, the contractor took his leave.

"However, as I think back on it" John says, "one minor thing did happen just as the contractor was leaving. Right by the door we had a large crock and in it was an antique walking stick that had been my grandfather's. The contractor had just said goodbye and as I was turning to go back into the living room, I heard a loud crack. I turned and saw that the walking stick was leaning half out of the crock, snapped in two like a twig. There was no one else in the room so I could not see how it could have happened. On top of that, this was a solid oak stick maybe an inch thick. Later I tried to snap the rest of it myself and couldn't. It sure was strange."

Strange though the incident might be, it was just the prelude for what was to come. The manifestations began to pick up in scope and intensity later that night. As the family was having dinner, suddenly a loud slap was heard and Brenda, seated at the end of the table, yelled out in pain and snapped her face to one side. Almost immediately, a large red welt appeared on her face. A moment later a platter of meat on the table neatly flipped over, spraying juice on Brenda.

Shortly thereafter, two pictures on the wall behind John fell violently to the floor and were smashed to bits. "I remember the pictures falling," says Mary. "It was not that they just fell–it was like they flew off the wall as though someone had tugged on them hard."

By now convinced that something truly peculiar was afoot, the family finished dinner quickly and was clearing the table when, in front of all present, a gravy boat scooted the length of the table and fell to the floor, once more splashing Brenda with gravy. Both Brenda and Amy now grew hysterical and John led the entire family into the living room. "I sat them down and said, 'Look, something really weird is going on here and if anyone knows anything about it, I want to know right now.' Both girls were crying and swearing that they had no idea what was causing this stuff and so we all just sort of hugged and then I think Mary said a prayer.

I had no idea what to do next. So I just said that we were all going to stay together in the living room"

During that evening and in the ensuing night, the manifestations continued unabated. Dozing on the couch later that evening, John was rudely awakened by a book flying off an adjacent shelf and hitting him on the head. First Brenda and then Amy reported the feeling of being pinched or poked by an unseen force. At one point during the evening, the family's attention was drawn to the kitchen, where they found a cupboard door had flown open and about twenty cans of food had been unceremoniously dumped onto the kitchen floor five feet away.

"It was sure crazy stuff," Mary remembers with an ironic smile. "I told John that maybe the house was possessed and suggested calling a priest but... where do you find a priest ready to do an exorcism at nine o'clock at night?"

Interestingly, as is typical in such cases, the disturbances seemed to center around Brenda. Most of the odd events seemed to occur when she was in the vicinity, though how she could be responsible for them seemed unclear at best. "Both John and I thought at first that maybe Brenda was doing this for some strange reason," Mary says, "but when these things started really happening, it was very clear to me that she could not be doing them all. How could a sixteen-year-old girl knock pictures off of the wall or slide a gravy boat off the table from six feet away?"

For her part, Brenda seemed as troubled as the rest of the family by the disturbances around her, particularly since she seemed to be the victim of most of the poltergeist's attention. Normally quiet and docile, the girl seemed to withdraw further into herself as the frightening manifestations continued, alternating between silence and hysterical sobbing.

Despite the inexplicable disturbances occurring around him, John still clung to the belief that some natural force was at work. However, even he had to agree that help was needed later than night when, once more, the sound of an explosion rocked the house, this time coming from a hallway next to the living room. "It was about eleven o'clock and I had been sleeping in an easy chair when it went off," John remembers, " and I ran to the hallway and found that a heavy oak bureau we had there as a hall table had been thrown over onto its side. I moved that bureau into the house in the first place and I can tell you it probably weighed a hundred pounds at least and yet it was clear on the other side of the hall." Now realizing that something must be done, John resorted to the only recourse that seemed left to him and called the Kokomo police department.

Simply reporting "a disturbance" at the home, John asked that an officer immediately be sent and about five minutes later, two police cars arrived at the home. As John and Mary explained to the police what had been occurring, both officers stared at the Spurnings in frank disbelief. Then, while one officer stayed with the family in the living room, his partner made a careful inspection of the home. "Both of the policemen were polite" Mary recalls, "but we could tell they did not believe us. As the one officer talked with us, he began to sort of hint that maybe the girls were just playing pranks on us. We told him that we did not think they were capable of doing all the things we had been seeing, but he was skeptical to say the least."

Finally, the second officer returned and reported that he could find nothing amiss in the home. He then asked to speak to John Spurning privately in the hall. No doubt it was his intention to further cast the shadow of doubt on Brenda's innocence in the matter, but in the end he never got that opportunity.

As the officer later reported the incident to a friend, "We got out in the hall and I started to walk back toward the kitchen when suddenly someone or something shoved me hard from one side of the hallway toward the other. It was a violent push. I hit the other wall and turned around, reaching for my gun, but there was no one there. The owner of the home was a good seven feet behind me."

Now the officer too began to suspect something strange was going on in the home. With his partner, he again toured the house top to bottom, carefully inspecting every closet and even entering the attic to look for some explanation, but none afforded itself. Further, while walking through the kitchen, they too heard the knocking on the wall that had begun the manifestations a few weeks before. They carefully checked both sides of the wall, yet while the knocking continued no source could be found. Some two hours later, the officers left the home, reluctantly telling John and Mary Spurning that they could not help them. They then returned to their station, opting not to file an official report on an incident neither could comprehend.

Meanwhile, back at the Spurning home, the havoc continued. After the officers left their home, John found himself once more walking the main floor hallway on his way toward the kitchen. As he did so, his attention was drawn toward the main bathroom in the hall. Now ready for nearly anything, John opened the door to the bathroom to find the shower running full force and the faucets in the sink turned on as well. After quickly looking around, John turned both faucets off, yet as he did so, he was disturbed to still hear the sound of running water, this time from the upstairs section of the home. He next went to an upstairs bathroom to find the water in both the sink and bathtub running as well. Turning these off, John returned once more to the main floor and found the water in the downstairs bathroom turned on once again.

Such was the state of affairs in the Spurning home for the next three days. Twice more the police were called in to investigate and twice more officers left baffled by the seemingly inexplicable incidents. At one point, the local fire department was called in when a foul odor suddenly filled the lower section of the home. Fearing a gas leak, John called local authorities, but shortly before the firemen arrived, the smell disappeared suddenly.

All the while the regular routine of knocks, explosions and moving objects continued. At one point during an evening, John was in the living room watching television while his daughter Amy slept on a couch opposite him and Brenda sat in a nearby chair. As John glanced over at his sleeping daughter, he was shocked to see one end of the couch slowly rise from the floor to a distance of about three inches and remain there for several seconds before gently returning to its original position.

During this period of time, Brenda became increasingly withdrawn and silent. Because it was apparent that most of the manifestations occurred while she was in the room, or at least nearby, Brenda understood that she might be considered a suspect and this further drove her into herself. Interestingly, the more she withdrew from conversation, the stronger and more frequent the disturbances seem to become.

After three days during which Brenda refused to leave the home despite the strange occurrences tormenting her, John and Mary decided the that girl needed professional help. A psychologist who specialized in the treatment of adolescents was contacted and a consultation with John and Mary was arranged. During their visit with the doctor, the Spurnings chose to be frank with him about what was happening in their home and to his credit the doctor seemed open to believe what they had to say. An appointment was made for Brenda to see the doctor the next afternoon.

The morning before Brenda's first appointment the manifestations reached their climax. All morning, knockings and the sound of explosions rocked the home. Glasses shattered in kitchen cabinets and a cane rocker in the living room was reduced to splinters by an unseen force. However, after Brenda returned from her appointment that afternoon, the manifestations seemed to weaken slightly.

During the next several weeks, Brenda continued to visit with the counselor, learning to open up and release some of the emotional tension with which she had been living. Interestingly, during that time the phenomena seemed to dwindle in frequency and strength. Odd tappings did continue to sound from the walls of the home at irregular intervals and Brenda twice more reported being slapped and shoved against walls. Yet by the end September the manifestations had ceased. Brenda continued to visit her counselor weekly for another two months, but for the rest of her year-long stay, the Spurning home remained peaceful and quiet. Whatever terrible force had erupted in their home had spent its fury and gone. The poltergeist was heard of no more.

Today, the events of over twenty years ago are only a bizarre memory in the minds of John and Mary Spurning. Their niece Brenda is now a registered nurse with a career in the Air Force. Although John and Mary remain in contact with her, they have never spoken again of the strange experience that so disturbed their lives. "Perhaps some things are best left buried and forgotten," John concludes.

* * *

As extraordinary and inexplicable as the events in the Spurning home may be, they are by no means the only time the Hoosier state has been the site of a poltergeist visitation. In April 1941 the small town of Odon became the site of even more destructive manifestations which briefly came to national attention.

Of all of the various activities attributed to poltergeists, perhaps the most devastating and dramatic is the sudden and unexplained appearance of fire. Cases of so-called "spontaneous immolation" have been reported for hundreds of years. While many have been explained as the work of vandals or arsonists, some spontaneous fires have defied logic or explanation. Such cases often involve the sudden appearance of an intense fire that sometimes completely consumes an object or even a person, yet leaves nearby surroundings untouched and unscorched. Although rare, investigators have, for many years, puzzled over such cases of unexplained combustion.

Such a case began in Odon, Indiana, at the farm of William Hackler one early spring day in 1941.[1] The day began as usual for the Hackler family. Since the weather was unseasonably warm, Mr. Hackler rose early to begin the day's planting. Just after eight o'clock, as the family was finishing clearing the breakfast table and Mr. Hackler was headed toward the barn, the smell of smoke began to filter down to the main floor from the upstairs section of the house. The family frantically ran upstairs and began a search for the source of the smoke and discovered a small blaze in the wall of an upstairs bedroom.

Immediately the local fire department was called, and in a short while they arrived and with little trouble extinguished the smoldering fire. With the fire dead, the firemen left the Hackler farm, no doubt feeling the satisfaction of a job well done. As it turned out, however, this particular job would no be so easily dispensed with.

Shortly after returning to their fire station, the firemen received a call to return to the farm. A second fire had been discovered, this time in a mattress in another bedroom. When they arrived, they were shocked to further discover the smoky fire burning *within* the feather mattress, rather than on the outside. It seemed as though the feathers inside of the mattress had been set ablaze from the inside, without any cut or tear in the mattress cover to account for its presence. That mattress was dragged outside and doused with water, and the flames were extinguished. As one volunteer fireman later told a local paper, "It was like the fire was completely contained in the mattress–there was no way you could set a fire like that."

Before the firemen could return to town once again, more fires were discovered. Located all throughout the house, the fires seemed to erupt spontaneously in areas where no one had been present before. No sooner had one fire been put out than another two fires were found. All told, nine fires were discovered on the farm by eleven o'clock that morning.

At one point, a fireman walking through the family living room noticed smoke emanating from a bookshelf. Picking up a volume, he found the book burning from within, yet the cover of the book remained unscorched.

A short time later, a fireman sitting at the kitchen table taking a brief break from his work was chagrined to see Mr. Hackler's overalls, hanging on a hook by the back door, suddenly erupt in flames. Before he could rush to the door to investigate, they were reduced to ashes in a moment's time.

By two o'clock that afternoon, firemen from two adjoining counties had joined in the effort and by all accounts they had their hands full. An amazing total of twenty-eight separate fires were discovered in the house in one day. No room of the home was spared from a fire. It was only due to the dedicated work of these volunteers that the house was spared from complete destruction. Amazingly it was not seriously damaged by the barrage of strange combustion.

By three o'clock, the fires had ceased as suddenly and mysteriously as they had begun. Peace once more returned to the farm and the firemen went on their way, tired and perplexed. However, enough was enough for Mr. Hackler. Moving his family's beds to the back yard, he, his wife and children slept the night in the open. Better to suffer the chill of the night air than to risk a return of the strange force that might turn their home to an inferno at will. The Hacklers never again slept in their home. The next day they moved to the home of Mrs. Hackler's sister. A week later Mr. Hackler tore the house down, salvaged the lumber and with the help of friends and neighbors built another home several miles away. There they lived for many years, unmolested by what had become known in the area as "the fire poltergeist."

Despite much speculation and subsequent investigation, no explanation for the fires at the Hackler farm has ever been given. At first, the children of the home were suspected of setting the blazes, yet the sheer number of fires that erupted so quickly in a house literally filled with firemen argued against such an assumption. Today, faulty electrical wiring might be pointed to as a possible cause, yet at the time the Hackler farm had not been wired for electricity.

One local reporter later theorized that the farm might be located in the center of "an unknown magnetic field" that had somehow endued the house with a strange energy. Yet no such magnetic field could be verified. Still another theory suggested that an old well located under the house had leaked natural gas into the home, causing the spontaneous eruptions, yet the home had never before exhibited the signs of such gas.

In the end, despite many theories and much consideration, the Odon Fires, as they came to be known, remain a mystery. The official report of police termed the fires a "most baffling mystery." The final note on the fires came several months later when the Travelers Insurance Company, which had insured the Hackler home, placed a full page ad in the April 19, 1941, edition of *Colliers* magazine. Describing the perplexing incident, the advertisement proudly claimed that the company had paid the Hacklers for the damage to their home. As was pointed out in the advertisement, they had insured the family against fire–*any* kind of fire!

Today, the subject of poltergeist phenomena is still studied and debated among parapsychologists and psychical researchers. Skeptics explain away all such incidents as the pranks of children and outright fraud. However, if one were to ask some residents of the Hoosier state about such an explanation, they would scoff. After all, they had seen, heard and sometimes felt something that cannot be as easily explained as a prank. They have felt the fury of the legendary poltergeist and while they, like we, may never understand such phenomena, they know them to be real.

10
Little Girl Lost
Schrererville, Indiana

From the first moment Bob and Nancy Frazee saw the old house in Schererville, they knew that it would be theirs. Something in the charm and quiet dignity of the old home simply claimed them.

Bob and Nancy, both natives of the south side of Chicago, had been looking for a house that would allow room for their growing family and the comparatively uncongested area of northwest Indiana appealed to them. Moreover, when their real estate agent showed them the large old home, they fell in love with it. True, the home was empty and badly in need of repair, but this was hardly an insurmountable obstacle for Bob, who had worked in construction for most of his life. Besides, the home was roomy enough for them and their five children and the price was right.

"I still vividly remember walking through the house for the first time," Nancy says. "The rooms were musty smelling and there was wallpaper hanging off the walls. It obviously had not been lived in for a long time but as we walked through, something about the place just made me fall in love with it. Halfway through our tour, I took Bob aside, looked him square in the eye and said, 'I want this house.' It was that simple. He agreed."

Bob and Nancy made an offer that day and a week later they took possession. Due to the need for repairs before the house could be made livable, they decided to continue to stay in their rented house in Illinois for the next several months while Bob would work nights and weekends renovating the house. There was much to be done.

"The house had two stories and five bedrooms and the whole place had been neglected for a long time," Bob says. "I had to replace the drywall in most of the house as well as updating the plumbing and electrical work. We bought the house in April of 1959 and all summer, I worked myself nearly to death getting it in shape."

During this time Bob got his first indication that there might be an unseen and uninvited tenant in the home. "It was a Saturday afternoon and I was working on the wall next to the staircase," Bob recalls. "Two of my sons had been working with me that day finishing the drywall but I had sent them home with their mother about an hour before. As I stood on the stairs sanding off the spackle, I heard this voice close behind me. It sounded like a little girl and she just called out 'Mommy!' but there was something in her voice that made the hair on my arms stand up. She sounded sad–almost lost."

Thinking that a child had wandered into the home. Bob spun on his heel to find the space behind him empty. A quick check of both floors revealed that he was apparently alone in the home. "I began to think that I was going a little nuts," Bob says with a grin. "Maybe all those hours of work and too little sleep were finally catching up with me. So I looked around again, made sure the front door was locked and went back to work. But about five minutes after I went back to sanding, I heard it again–a little girl's voice just behind me calling for her mommy. I have to tell you, I was spooked. So after I looked around again, I quickly got my supplies and left."

Deciding not to mention the incident to his wife out of fear of upsetting her, Bob returned home and spent an enjoyable evening with his family. During the next week, however, Bob would return daily to the old house after work to continue his renovations. Nothing out of the ordinary occurred for the next week or so and he began to think that perhaps the extraordinary event had been a product of his imagination after all.

However, in early August another incident occurred that made him question that assumption. "It was in the evening, about eight o'clock or so and I had been working on the house since I got off work at two," Bob says. "I was in the kitchen taking a break, smoking a cigarette, when I heard something scamper across the floor of the bedroom directly above me. It sounded like light footsteps, like a child would make. Then I heard something like a ball bouncing and a little girl's giggle. I thought to myself 'Holy smokes, here we go again!' and then I started for the stairs."

Entering the bedroom from which he had heard the sounds, Bob found the room dark and empty. "The one thing that did strike me, though," he adds, "was the fact that the room was cold. It was a hot night and the rest of the home was sweltering, but that room was cold. It gave me the creeps. I decided right then and there it was time to go home."

Quickly retracing his steps, Bob made his way through the dark house to the downstairs kitchen to pick up his wallet, which he had left on the table. Taking it, Bob found his keys and was in the process of leaving through the back door when the by-now familiar voice beckoned to him from the dark living room. "It was that same voice of a little girl calling out 'Mommy?' " Bob recalls. "I was not sure just what to do but I knew that I was alone in the house so I just shut the door and walked to my car."

On the way home Bob thought over the disturbances that he had experienced in the house. Clearly the idea that the house might be inhabited by some sort of unseen presence was one he was not prone to believe. As a pragmatic man, his mind rejected the idea of ghosts or spirits. Yet he could not deny the fact that something was going on which seemed to defy logical explanation. Moreover, something in the nature of the manifestations was upsetting for Bob. Though a gruff, burly construction worker, Bob was a loving father and the idea of a child being alone in the dark and calling for her mother brought him a sense of sadness. "I am a dad, after all," Bob says, "and it upset me to hear a child calling for her mother and apparently not finding her." Still Bob refused to tell his family about the events. "I just did not want to scare them, that's all," he says.

During the next several weeks, the manifestations came again and again. At one point while working in an upstairs bedroom with his teenage son John, both heard the sound of a regular squeaking coming from the attic above them. Bob tried to ignore the sounds, but after a few minutes, he glanced at his son who was staring at the ceiling above them. Wide-eyed, John looked at his father and said, "What is it, Dad?"

"I don't know–mice maybe," Bob replied, trying to sound nonchalant. Telling his son to stay in the room, Bob went downstairs to find a ladder and, returning to the upper floor, opened a panel in the ceiling, and entered the attic.

"By then the sound had stopped but I looked around the attic with my flashlight. I had been there once before, checking the roof for leaks, but I had not really seen what was up there. It was basically empty but in one corner something caught my eye. It was a small antique rocking horse. It was covered with dust, like everything else in the attic, but as I walked over to it I saw something that startled me. Even though the horse was dust covered, the seat and hand grips were clean, like someone had just been sitting on it. Then, I slowly reached out and rocked that horse forward. It made a squeaking sound just like we had been hearing downstairs."

"I shook my head and went down to my son. When I got there he asked me what had caused the noise but I just looked at him and said it was mice. I don't think he believed me, but I just told him to get back to work. He did not say much more the rest of that day."

By the end of August, the main work in the home was nearly completed and the family prepared to move into the newly refurbished home. During the last week before moving day, Bob and Nancy asked Bob's parents to stay with their children, allowing them to stay at the house and work steadily in order to finish the work. It was then that Nancy first became aware of the ghostly presence there.

" I will never forget that night," Nancy says. "We had been working like crazy all day and by 5:00 I was too tired to cook, so Bob said he would go pick up some food at a nearby restaurant and bring it back. He had been gone about five minutes and I was cleaning up the kitchen when suddenly I head the sound of footsteps coming down the stairs from the second floor. It was a child's steps and they sort of skipped down the stairs.

"I was startled, to say the least, and I stared into the living room, waiting to see if someone would come in, but no one was there. After a minute, I walked to the living room and looked up the stairs but no one was to be seen. I thought I was going crazy. Then I heard a sigh coming close to my ear. A flood of emotion ran through me–I was frightened, but there was another emotion there too. It was like a deep sadness. It almost felt like someone had reached out and touched me."

Suddenly finding herself in tears, Nancy ran back to the kitchen and sat at the table drinking coffee. "It was probably no more than fifteen minutes till Bob came back but it felt like an hour," she remembers. "He walked in the back door and saw me sitting there crying and asked me what was the matter. I looked up at him and stammered something about hearing footsteps and before I could say anything more he looked at me and said 'So you heard her too.' Then he sat down and put his arm around me."

Nancy and Bob spoke for several hours that night and Bob told his wife about what he had heard and experienced in the home. While initially angry that her husband had not told her of what was going on, in the end both agreed that they should not tell their children about the spectral activity in the home. "I could not imagine how my children would react," Nancy says.

For the remaining days of that week, Bob and Nancy stayed in their new home, working nearly around the clock to get it prepared for them to move in the next Saturday. During that time, the strange occurrences continued.

"They were never anything evil or destructive," Nancy remembers almost fondly. "At their worst, they were annoying–like a naughty child playing games with you."

Several times odd sounds were heard in the home. Twice Nancy was awakened in the middle of the night by the eerie sounds of the antique rocking horse squeaking from the attic, and almost daily, the sound of a child's laugh would be heard coming from some odd corner of the house. "I began to get terrified" Nancy says, "but I knew that we had bought this house and we were not about to give up on it."

As the week wore on, even more inexplicable events began to occur. One morning, Bob, painting a bathroom cupboard, stepped out into the hall for a moment, and returned to see the paint overturned in the middle of the bathtub. After he had cleaned up the mess, he went to examine his work and found a single child's thumbprint in the drying paint on the front of the cupboard. "It was right where you could not miss it," Bob says. "I think she really wanted me to find it."

Several times during the week Nancy was startled to her a child's voice calling for her mother. Like her husband, she reacted to the sound with a mixture of both fear and compassion. "The voice was what really got to me," she recalls. "It was both scary and heartbreaking. I had little ones too and just as Bob said, the thought of a little girl looking for her mommy was upsetting to me.

Another chilling occurrence happened late one morning after Nancy had finished patching holes in the plaster in an upstairs hallway. "I had been using a plaster trowel," she says, "and so the first thing I did was to go down to the kitchen and wash it out in the sink. I cleaned up the trowel and put it on the counter next to the sink. Just then I heard Bob, who was in the garage in the back, call for me so I went out the back door to help him."

When Nancy returned a few minutes later, she intended to dry the trowel and put it away but, mysteriously, it was no longer on the counter. According to Nancy, "I looked and looked, but it was nowhere around. I kept on telling myself that it had to be there somewhere, but it had vanished. Then I happened to think that it was getting late and that I should start making lunch. I glanced up at the clock we had over the doorway and I think my heart stopped."

There, carefully balanced along the top of the clock, some six feet from the floor, was the trowel. "I let out a yell that brought Bob running from the garage," she says, grinning. "He came through the door thinking the house had exploded and stared at me, but all I could do was just point up to the clock. He stared at it for a long minute and then I remember he turned to me and smiled. 'I guess our little girl wants to play,' he said and then he started laughing."

As strange as Bob's reaction might seem, it was a turning point for the couple. "I just decided at that point to quit being scared of this thing and to just accept it," Bob recalls. "If we were going to live around a spook, we might as well all be friends." For the rest of the week, when odd things occurred, Bob and Nancy began to simply try to shrug them off with a laugh or joke. Bob even took to occasionally talking to the little girl.

"When we went to bed one night, I turned off the light and lay down in bed and after a minute, I heard that damn squeaking from the attic." Bob says. "Nancy turned to me and said 'What are we going to do about that?' so I thought like a father and then called out loudly 'It's late. We are both tired. Now stop it this minute and go to bed or wherever you go!' In a second the squeaking stopped and we did not hear anything more that night."

By the end of the week, Bob and Nancy had become almost accustomed to their unseen visitor but both still worried about what might happen if their children became aware of her presence. "I pictured myself with five hysterical kids," Nancy says. "But we still did not think that we should tell them about it. No use getting them worked up before they had even settled in."

On Saturday of that week, Bob and Nancy moved their five children into their new home. For the first few days, the house resounded with the happy sounds of boxes being moved, beds being set up and children laughing as they explored their new home. During that time, no one seemed to notice anything out of the ordinary and the Frazees were both greatly relieved. Nancy even dared to hope that perhaps the spectral child had been driven out by the five very live ones. However, that was not to be the case.

The first hint Nancy had that something strange was still present in the home came one morning about a week after the family had settled into their new home. Their seven-year-old daughter Karen came down for breakfast and complained that someone had been playing with her dollhouse when she wasn't looking. When asked to explain what she meant, Karen reported that every night before going to bed, she would carefully arrange her doll house in perfect order and, shutting the door on the back of the house, would leave it for the night.

However, by the next morning she would find the dollhouse opened and its furniture rearranged. Nancy tried to suggest to her daughter that perhaps she had just forgotten to straighten the house the night before but her daughter was insistent, so Nancy let the matter drop. Later that week, however, Karen once again found her room disturbed.

"We had gone shopping for school clothes and when we came home Karen ran upstairs to try on a new outfit, but in a minute she was back downstairs looking mad," Nancy remembers. "I asked her what the problem was and she said that one of the other kids had gotten into her closet and left all of her clothes on the floor. I went with her to look and sure enough, all of her dresses were off their hangers and lying on the floor of the closet. A few were even in the room, like someone had tried them on and then threw them down. I immediately assembled all of the other kids, but they all swore they had not been in the room all morning."

Soon the other Frazee children began to notice odd things about their new home too. Thirteen-year-old Rob came to his father to report a baseball missing from his room. A prized memento (it was autographed by Don Kessenger of the Chicago Cubs), Rob turned his room upside down looking for it but it was nowhere to be found. He had all but given up hope of ever finding it when one night about at midnight, the boy was awakened from his sleep by the feeling of something being dropped on his bed. He sat up to find his prized baseball lying on the foot of the bed. The next morning, his brothers and sisters all denied any knowledge of the ball's disappearance or mysterious reappearance.

Still, despite the odd occurrences, none of the Frazee children seemed aware of anything supernatural in the house until the point was driven home to the Frazee's eldest son John on a Saturday afternoon. "That's one time I'll never forget," Bob says. "It was late Saturday afternoon and we were supposed to go visit relatives the next day, so Nancy declared that we were all going to Saturday afternoon mass at the Catholic Church down the street. She got all the kids dressed except John, who said he wanted to work on his room and did not want to go. He and his mother had a few rounds about that, but in the end she said he could stay home this once if he wanted to."

"We all went to mass and got home at about 5:30. I remember it had started to rain, and when I pulled into the driveway I saw John huddled in the back next to the garage. He was just standing there all wet and looking really shaken. My first thought was, 'Oh boy, what did he do now?'" Climbing out of the car, Bob and Nancy went to their son and asked him what he was doing out in the rain. At first, the boy refused to say much, but when his mother ordered him back into the house he refused saying, "Mom, I don't think I want to go back in the house–ever!"

By now Bob and Nancy had an idea that something strange was occurring and coaxed their son back into the living room of the home. Herding the rest of the children to their rooms, out of earshot, they calmed the shaken boy and asked him what had happened "The first thing he said to me was, 'Dad, your not going to believe me,'" Bob says, "but I looked him in the eye and said, 'Try me–you might be surprised.' Then he told me that after we left, he had gone up to his room to begin rearranging his furniture when suddenly he heard footsteps in the hall. He said he looked out, saw that no one was there, and decided that he had just imagined it, so, he shut his door and went back to work. In a minute, though, he heard this little girl's voice come from the hall pleading 'Mommy!' "

By now frightened, John had locked the door to his room and turned on all the lights. Sitting on his bed, he was unsure of what to do next when the voice came again calling out "Mommy!" more insistently. However, now the voice was in the room with him.

"I had never seen my son so shaken." Nancy says. "He was a big boy at sixteen- a football player and not sacred of anything, but he told us that when he heard that voice in the room with him, he was sacred to death."

Throwing open his door, John went running through the house toward the nearest door. As he moved through the house, the voice seemed to follow him, twice more calling out its single utterance before he flung open the back door and ran for the garage. Finding the garage locked, John elected to stand in the rain rather than risk returning to the house and whatever waited there.

After hearing their son's tale, the Frazee's knew that they had to talk to their children about what was happening in their home. "Bob went upstairs to get the rest of the kids for a family meeting," Nancy remembers, "and I sat there on the couch consoling John. I did not want to have this talk with the kids. I had no idea how they would react."

In fact, when Bob and Nancy did tell their children about what had been happening in the home, stressing that nothing hurtful or evil had happened, they were shocked by their children's reaction.

"They were delighted," Bob says. "Even the little ones. Karen jumped up and down and said, "We have a ghost! We have a ghost! This is *so* cool!" Immediately one of the other children asked if they could turn their new home into a real 'haunted house' for Halloween and several remarked that they could not wait to go to there new school and tell their friends–an idea that Nancy discouraged. After a while, even John regained his calm and began to get into the spirit of the thing.

"When we were done with our talk, I realize that I felt a good deal better," Bob says, "but I also had this crazy idea that there was something else I needed to do too. I had to have a talk with that little girl. But how do you get in touch with a spook?"

As it turned out, Bob would have just such an opportunity a few days later. "It was about five o'clock in the morning and I was the only one up," he recalls. "I was sitting at the kitchen table drinking coffee and having a cigarette when I heard that same voice from close by me calling, 'Mommy!' At first I felt a chill run down my back and then I turned in the direction of the voice and calmly said, 'Honey, your mommy isn't here. She doesn't live here anymore, but we do. Now we are willing to let you stay here and to be your family but you have to try to not scare the children. We want to get along, OK?' Then, I swear I felt the room got brighter. I left that morning and nothing really frightening ever happened again."

From that day on, while the manifestations continued, the Frazees and their children were never more made to feel uncomfortable. "I know it sounds crazy, but we just sort of accepted her as a part of our family." Nancy says. In fact, the Frazees and their children began to go out of their way to make the spirit feel at home. Karen began to purposely leave her dollhouse open at night in order to let the spirit know it was welcome. Some of the children would occasionally call a goodnight to 'their' ghost, whom they named Elizabeth in honor of a maiden aunt. "I hate to admit it, but even I got in on it a little," Nancy says. "When I would get home in the middle of the day when the kids and Bob were gone, I would come in through the back door and yell 'Don't worry Elizabeth, it's just me!' "

It was also at Nancy's suggestion that Bob brought the antique rocking horse down from its place in the attic, dusted it off, and set it in a place of honor in the living room. "It almost became a family joke," Bob says. "When the girls got older and would bring a boyfriend home to meet us, the boy would notice the rocker and someone would say 'Oh, that belongs to our ghost.' "

Perhaps the rocker still did belong to the spirit, as evidenced by the fact that on several mornings, when leaving early for work, Bob would come down the stairs to the living room to see the rocker slowly moving, as though someone had just gotten through riding it.

Bob and Nancy Frazee are not alone in remembering this time fondly. Karen, now a physical therapist in Chicago, remembers the ghost with affection as well. "I guess that I thought of her as a little sister, only a sister I couldn't see," she says ironically. "The one incident I really remember was when I was about eleven and a friend was over. We were playing in the kitchen. Mom had been making a pie and so there was flour all over the counter top."

"We were making shapes and drawing in the flour when my mom called us out into the living room for something. When we got back, we saw that a set of handprints had been added to ours in the flour. But these were smaller than either of ours - we checked. My friend got scared and looked at me but I just told her it was our ghost and not to worry. Then I cleaned up the flour and was done with it," she concludes with a smile.

Indeed the spirit of the little girl did seem to become a valued member of the family. At one point young Matt even suggesting that a place be set for her at the table for Thanksgiving, but the suggestion was immediately overruled by Nancy. "I did not want another set of dishes to wash!" she explains. Interestingly, however, the true identity of the child's spirit was never known. At one point in the 1970s, Nancy went to the county court-house and looked for records on the inhabitants of the house, but none could be found beyond the previous owners, who, she knew, had been childless. Neighbors did not recall ever hearing of a death in the house and in the end Nancy gave up her quest to know the identity of the spirit. Instead, she, like the other members of her family, just settled in and ac-cept the playful spirit as a part of their lives, unseen yet felt. For the rest of their many years there, the Frazees came to love their home and love whatever spirit dwelt there as one of their own.

Although the Frazees lived in the home for thirty years, they never actually saw the spirit. The only possible sighting of the ghost came from a neighbor who saw Nancy Frazee one Sunday morning in the narthex of their church. "This sweet elderly lady from down the street met me on the way out of church," Nancy says, "and she said to me 'I see you have a relative visiting you my dear. Is she enjoying her visit?' I was a little taken aback and I asked her just what she meant."

"She told me that she had walked by the house the week before and saw a little girl staring out of an upstairs window. She described her as wearing a dress and having curly blond hair. I smiled and said 'Yes, that is a member of the family. And I do think she is enjoying her visit.' "

In 1989, Bob and Nancy Frazee, now alone, reluctantly sold their beloved home. After their children had left the house, the manifestations quieted down but their resident spirit still occasionally made its presence known. It was with a deep sense of sadness that they entrusted her and their home to the new tenants.

"I cried when we put it on the market," Nancy says, "but when we got a visit from the family who had made an offer on the house, I did feel a bit better. They were a nice young couple with three children of their own, one a girl of about eight. I thought our little girl might like that."

"When they walked into the living room the mother looked over at the antique rocking horse and said 'Oh that is beautiful! I love that horse!' I smiled and told her it had been with the house when we bought it and I thought that should stay with the house if it was OK with her. She loved the idea and said it would remain where it was. I almost added that there was something else that was staying with the house, too, but thought better of it. They could find out about our little girl on their own."

Perhaps they have, or perhaps the little girl has gone her own way. Maybe the love and compassion shown her by a loving family has finally set her free from the bonds of life and finally given her peace.

11
The Spirited Guests of French Lick Springs Resort
French Lick, Indiana

Indiana can boast of a great many opulent and comfortable hotels and vacation spots. From luxurious downtown hotels to rustic bed and breakfast inns, the Hoosier state is dotted with striking examples of Midwest hospitality and comfort. Of all such resorts, however, none can truly compare to the splendor and grandeur of the French Lick Springs Grand Hotel, located in French Lick, Indiana.

Situated in the rolling beauty of the 2,600 acre Hoosier National Forest, the French Lick Grand Hotel is at once historic and sweeping in its beauty. Boasting of over a hundred years of service, the hotel is a sweeping complex, offering 485 guestrooms, an 800-seat convention hall and a 2,500-hundred seat exhibition hall, where major concerts are regularly scheduled.

Priding itself as a resort that offers all the amenities, the hotel features two superb golf courses, as well as badminton, volleyball, horseshoes, shuffleboard, croquet, horse stables, bowling alleys and a game room. There are two swimming pools, in addition to tennis courts and mineral baths, which are offered with professional massages.

A massive ballroom seats over 800 and is the site of the hotel's yearly Halloween masquerade ball. Ornate woodwork adorns the interior of the hotel as well as high ceilings with beautiful chandeliers throughout the massive building. Walking through the doors of this graceful old resort is like taking a step back through time.

Such an impression is not altogether inappropriate since the hotel and the countryside that surrounds it are rich in history. French traders first settled the area called French Lick, Indiana, site of the French Lick Springs Resort and established one of the earliest outposts in the middle-western wilderness, more than 200 years ago.

After the discovery of rich mineral springs, which attracted animals that flocked to lick the waters and wet rocks, this valley became known among settlers as "the Lick." The French had ideas about exploiting these lush salt deposits, but because of one obstacle and another (not the least of which was relentless harassment by Indians) they never did make much progress. Finally, following the Louisiana Purchase Treaty in 1803, in which Napoleon relinquished claims on that part of the frontier, the French abandoned their trading posts at the Lick.

British settlers moved in about 1812 and despite continued Indian resistance, they succeeded in establishing a permanent fort. Indian incidents continued, however. One of the first recorded was the slaying of Irishman William Charles, who was bushwhacked by Indians outside the fort. His remains are rumored to be buried somewhere beneath the front lawn of the resort.

In 1832, all the lands surrounding the actual mineral springs, which had been reserved for production of salt, were offered for public sale. Lured by the potential profit to be made in the area, fifteen hundred acres (including all the large springs) were purchased by a Dr. William A. Bowles. Within several years he opened the first French Lick Springs Hotel, a ramshackle, three-story frame building. It was an immediate success. People flocked from hundreds of miles to partake of the "miracle waters". They carried the mineral water away in all sorts of jugs and canvas containers. "Doc" Bowles had struck it rich.

In the 1850s, as North-South tension mounted, French Lick was a key station of the Underground Railroad. To counter this activity, Doc Bowles, who had always indicated sympathy for the Southern cause, helped organize a Confederate secret society, called Knights of the Golden Circle. In 1857, however, Bowles did take time out from his subversive activities to help charter the town of French Lick.

Just before the Civil War, Bowles was arrested, court-martialed, convicted of treason and sentenced to death. President Lincoln, however, quietly commuted the sentence to life imprisonment. Bowles spent the war in a Federal prison in Ohio. He returned to French Lick in 1865 and managed the hotel until his death in 1873.

French Lick Springs thrived under various managements until 1897, when a disastrous fire destroyed most of the old frame buildings. Shortly thereafter the ruins were purchased by a syndicate, which called itself the French Lick Springs Hotel Company, headed by Thomas Taggart, then mayor of Indianapolis.

It was under Taggart's imaginative rule that French Lick Springs rocketed to international prominence. First he rebuilt a new main wing. He had the Monon Railroad lay a special spur and run daily trains between Chicago and the front entrance of the hotel. He later designed a championship golf course (still later, a second), as well as modernized and expanded the baths. The innovative owner also began bottling "Pluto Water" in concentrated form for national distribution. With an expansive and luxurious spa (and after Taggart had been named Democratic National Chairman in 1904), the elite of politics and society suddenly "discovered" French Lick Springs. It was at this hotel, too, in 1917, that a world famous

Photo: French Lick Springs Resort

The elegant gazebo at French Lick Springs Resort.

chef, Louis Perrin, first introduced tomato juice to the world.

Taggart insisted that the resort maintain a rigidly elegant dedication to health and recreation–although he was no teetotaler, he never permitted liquor on the premises. The first bar was not opened, in fact until after "repeal," some years following the old man's demise. The wealthy celebrities who descended upon the little town in the Indiana hills each spring and fall came to take "the cure," to play, to conduct business and to gamble.

Taggart always disclaimed any connection with plush gambling casinos throughout the valley. It never was officially explained, however, how, in flagrant violation of state law, two big gambling rooms operated across the street from the hotel, and perhaps half a dozen others catered to lesser hotel guests and common folk. In addition, at one time, there was even a combination dice room and bowling alley right in the middle of the hotel's own Japanese gardens, near the Pluto Spring. In any event, French Lick Springs was to become as well known for its resort facilities. The last casinos were shuttered in 1949. One of these buildings was taken over by the American Legion.

Taggart, who served briefly as a U.S. Senator by appointment, had three more wings added to the hotel in the next twenty years. Taggart, who described himself as a hotelman first and a political hobbyist second, grew in political stature until he was the acknowledged power behind Democratic politics in the U.S. Simultaneously, and French Lick Springs developed a reputation as the unofficial party headquarters. It was there in Taggart's hotel in 1931 that Franklin Roosevelt rounded up support at a Democratic governors' conference for his party's presidential nomination.

Tom Taggart died in 1929. His son (the only boy among six children), Thomas D. Taggart, carried on. With the Depression, however, the popular French Lick Springs Resort began to decline. World War II brought a monetary revival, but in 1946 young Tom Taggart sold out to a New York syndicate.

Several years ago the resort and its surrounding estate were acquired by Boykin Lodging Company, which spent several million dollars painstakingly restoring the beloved old building to its former splendor.

During its rich and colorful history, the French Lick Springs Resort has hosted a legion of the rich and famous, including John Barrymore,

Clark Gable, Bing Crosby, President Roosevelt, the Trumans, and the Reagans. They, along with a legion of lesser-known guests who have visited the opulent resort in the past hundred years, strolled in the lush rose gardens, sipped brandy in the parlor and relaxed in the mineral springs. In this beautiful and comfortable setting, they rested their bodies and rejuvenated their spirits.[1]

Perhaps, then, it is not so surprising that it is said that at least a few of the guests have chosen to remain behind at the resort, long after their mortal lives have passed. It has been whispered for many years that amid the grandeur and splendor of this beautiful resort, otherworldly spirits may well walk. Sometimes courteous and helpful, the ghosts of French Lick Springs Resort are a fascinating yet little known part of the heritage of this special place.

Perhaps the best known ghost in the resort is said to be that of former owner Thomas Taggart. This man spent his life and fortune in developing the French Lick Grand and is said to be responsible for much of the odd activity encountered in the hotel.

Several of these incidents seem to center around the old service elevator which is used to transport guests and baggage to the upper floors of the hotel. Always accommodating and helpful to both guests and employees, Taggart in his day was frequently known to enter the elevator first when a patron or bellhop was carrying in luggage and then to hold the door for them as they entered.

Such a benevolent habit might well be forgotten in the seventy years since his death were it not for the fact that, still today, employees struggling toward the service elevator with their arms full of luggage have been shocked to see the doors of that elevator open, apparently of their own volition and seem to be held open until they had entered the elevator.

One former employee, Jeremy Brown,* remembers such an incident distinctly. Brown, now an engineer with an Indianapolis company, grew up near French Lick and spent several enjoyable summers working at the resort. "When I first got the job, one of the other employees told me about Taggart's ghost but I just sort of laughed it off. I guess I thought they were just trying to scare a new guy. But after a while, I started to wonder.

"You walk those long corridors at night and it is easy to get spooked and wonder if you are not alone in the hallway," Brown continues. "Sometimes I would hear a noise that I could not explain but it could have been one of the guests just knocking around in their room. Anyway, I had just started to wonder about the stories when the incidents with the elevator happened. It is an old elevator and we used it particularly during the busy times to take guests' luggage up to their rooms.

"One summer afternoon I remember the hotel was just crazy with people checking in and out and I had my arms full of luggage as I walked toward the door. I was just about ready to put the luggage down to punch the button for the elevator when I saw the doors start to open. I stepped back, thinking someone was going to get off, but when the doors opened I could see that there was no one in the elevator. That was strange, let me tell you, but what was weird was that as soon as I got on the elevator the doors closed behind me. Normally you have to push a button to open the doors and another to shut them, but this time it was like someone was doing that for me. Just being helpful I guess."

Later that day, Jeremy mentioned the incident to some of his fellow employees and to his shock, none of his fellow workers seemed surprised. Indeed, one of his friends simply smiled and remarked, "That's no big deal. Mr. Taggart is helpful that ways some times."

This would not be Mr. Brown's last experience with the odd behavior of the elevator. Several weeks later, an even more mysterious event occurred. "Again, it was a really busy time. I went to the desk and picked up a set of bags and the clerk asked me to take them to the second floor. I walked up to the elevator and, sure enough, as I approached the doors

Photo: French Lick Springs Resort

Guests relaxing on the porch in the early days of French Lick Springs Resort.

they slid open once again. After the first time, I was not nearly as spooked so I just kind of looked around and got on. I pressed the bottom for the second floor and the elevator started up. However, when we got to the second floor the elevator kept right on going. I looked at the button and even though I knew I had hit the button for the second floor, the button for the third floor was lit up.

"I thought this was really weird and in a second when the doors opened for the third floor I was ready to push the button to go to the second floor again. Then I looked down and saw that the tags on the luggage had room 320 on them. I guess even though the desk clerk and I had gotten it wrong, old Mr. Taggart had saved me a trip by getting me to the right floor after all."

Many other employees are said to have encountered similar experiences with the service elevator. As one worker says, "We all know the stories, but I am not sure how many people have really seen it happen. When it does happen, we just sort of shrug and say it is Mr. Taggart being helpful again."

Other tales told concerning the elevator say that late at night, the elevator has been known to run between floors without anyone being in it. Others have reported the smell of pipe or cigar tobacco emanating from an unseen source within the elevator, even though no smoking is now allowed there. One frequently reported tale tells of an employee, entering the elevator one night, seeing a vaporous form in the corner of the elevator that seemed to vanish before her startled eyes.

Another even more bizarre tale is told of the spirit of the benevolent Mr. Taggart, this time concerning the main ballroom. According to hotel legend, in life Mr. Taggart an avid horseman, as well as a bit of a roguish practical joker, was known on occasion to ride his favorite mount down the long hallway leading to the double doors and into the main ballroom for sport. Usually this was done during the winter when few guests were in the hotel, yet such a daring exploit soon became legendary among hotel employees. What makes the story doubly interesting is the fact that in the past decades, workers in the ballroom have been surprised to hear the distinct "clops" of a horse coming down the hallway toward the ballroom, and a few have been said to see the shadowy form of a phantom horse and rider parading through the room.

While such sensational sightings cannot be verified and must be considered to be the stuff of legend, other stories regarding the hotel are not so easily dismissed. Indeed, if the spirit of Thomas Taggart does walk (or ride) the halls of French Lick Resort, then perhaps he is not the only specter present there.

It is said that other stories have surfaced in recent years of ghosts elsewhere in the hotel. Many of them are linked to the sixth floor. Marge Henderson*, an executive with the resort, says, "The sixth floor is really the most notorious floor for spirits." Over the years more than a few guests and employees have reported strange encounters there. While none have been malevolent or hurtful, the stories have become part of the tapestry of legend and lore at the venerable old resort.

It is said that many of the cleaning and maintenance staff are reluctant to go to the sixth floor after nightfall. Many have reported the feeling of a "presence" there and a few are said to have seen strange shadows in the corners of the hallway. One former cleaning staff member tells of plugging in her vacuum cleaner to sweep the main hallway carpet, only to be distracted by the sound of footsteps coming up behind her. She turned and found the hallway empty, yet as she stepped away from her sweeper to investigate, she was startled to hear the sweeper turn itself on. "There was no way that could happen," she now says, "but it did."

Others too are said to have heard footsteps in the empty halls of the sixth floor. One maintenance worker, carrying a bag of tools down the hallway, reported feeling a rush of cold air pass by him, followed a moment later by the sound of a woman's gentle laugh close to his ear. An inspection of the area showed it to be devoid of human presence.

An even odder circumstance was the account which came from a cleaning woman on the sixth floor who, according to legend, looked up from her chores in a sixth floor room to see the wispy face of a woman reflected back at her from a large mirror in the room. The cleaning woman, it is said, left the room quickly and refused to reenter it for any reason.

Ms. Henderson also tells the story of a guest from Cincinnati, staying on the sixth floor, who awoke one night to hear the sound of his child lying on a nearby bed, giggling uncontrollably. When he asked his son later what had caused his fit of mirth, the boy said he was awakened during the night to the sensation that someone was gently tickling him.

Perhaps the strangest of all the tales told of the sixth floor involves the inexplicable function of a phone located in one room there. According to Marge Henderson, it has been long noted that, often late at night, the main desk will see a phone call coming in from that room. When picked up, no one seems to be on the line. What makes this circumstance truly bizarre is that this often has occurred when no guest was present in the room.

According to Ms. Henderson, numerous times maintenance workers have been sent to the room to check out the errant behavior of the phone and indeed at one point the room was closed and the phone removed, yet still the phantom calls have continued. Then came a night when Ms. Henderson personally encountered the strange phenomenon herself.

"They told me about the phone calls when I started working here," she now says, "and I thought it was a joke–just a housekeeper messing around or something. So, one night, I decided to try it myself. I called the room, which was empty at the time, and it was busy. This was strange because no one was in the room. So I camped on the line and eventually it started ringing. Then, in a minute the phone was picked up, but no one answered. I could hear the air conditioner in the room, which had an odd squeaking sound, but no one was there. It was spooky.

"I remember it was late when this happened, so I left the hotel and went home. I did not know quite what to think about it, but that night...*it called me.* My phone rang several times and when I picked it up I could hear that odd squeaking sound, just like I had at the hotel, but no one was there."

Another former employer who worked in an office on the corridor also reports a similar experience, as well as the sound of a heavy cart being pushed past her doorway when no one was in the area.

Other odd tales, too, abound in the majestic resort. A desk clerk has reported hearing the bell on her desk, used to indicate when a patron needs service, being rung repeatedly when her back is turned. Invariably, when she turns toward the sound, the lobby is empty. Another former security worker tells of seeing a hazy white form walking past the dining room one night as he was closing the room. He gave chase but the form had disappeared.

Louise Conway*, an employee of the hotel, describes another incident that that implies a spirit presence in the hotel. "I was working in the theater one night" she remembers. "When they did evening shows it was my job to sit at a desk in the hallway and take tickets. Usually after a show began I would stay at the desk and take the tickets of anyone who would come in late for the performances. Well, this night the show had been going on for about twenty minutes and I was sitting there watching the show for my desk, when I heard the sound of someone walking around in the lobby which was just down the hallway. I turned and looked but there was no one there."

Passing off the event as nothing more than a strange trick of sound, Louise again turned her attention to the production in progress. Again she heard the sound of footsteps nearby. "It happened six or eight times, but there was no one there. Then, suddenly I felt someone take a finger, run it along the left side of my hair and touch my ear. I turned around, thinking that someone was fooling with me, but no one was there. I looked all over the area, even lifting a curtain to see if someone was hiding behind it, but I was alone. By now I was getting a little scared, but I made myself sit down. But in a minute I heard the footsteps again and then a second later I distinctly felt someone run their finger up along the left side of my hair a second time. Then I got up and ran to sit with the audience."

Later that night, sitting with some friends who had been present during the show, Louise was shocked when one woman turned to her and said, "Louise, did you have some trouble during the show tonight?"

Unsure of how to answer, Louise simply replied, "What do you mean?"

"I mean the man who was pacing around you there during the performance," came her reply. "We could see him from where we were sitting backstage. Who was he?" Her uncertainty now turned to fear, Louise told her friend the story of what had happened and assured her friend that whoever they had seen from a distance was invisible to her at the time.

The epilogue to this strange series of events came the next day when Louise returned to the lobby area of the convention hall to help with a short musical production. "On Saturdays the crew would come in to do fifteen minutes of song and dance for the guests and I would run the sound. On that day, my sister, who was the social director for the resort, was sitting across the lobby behind a desk watching the performance. After it was over, my sister came to me with this strange look on her face and said, 'Louise, you are not going to believe this, but as I was sitting there I know that I felt someone run their finger up along the left side of my hair and touch my ear.' I stared at her for a long minute and then I told her what had happened to me the night before."

It should be noted that none of the stories associated with the hotel are of a malign or evil nature. Indeed, most who speak of the phantoms said to inhabit the hotel do so in respectful and even fond terms. As one hotel housekeeper puts it "This is just such a beautiful old place...so serene and peaceful. I guess I just like to think that a few guests might have wanted to stick around. They aren't hurtful or mean; they are just...there. After all, if you had to pick a place to haunt, could you find more comfortable surroundings?"

Notes

Introduction:
[1] Patrick McManus, *The Good Samaritan Strikes Again.* Copyright 1992 by Patrick McManus

Chapter One: Two Very Different Marion Hauntings
[1] Mark Marimen; Personal Interviews and Research.

Chapter Two: The Ghost of the Missing Aviator
[1] Amelia Earhart, "Courage", appeared in Marion Perkin's *Survey Magazine*, July 1, 1928
[2] *American Magazine*, "Amelia Earhart's Scrapbook at Purdue University
[3] Morrissey, Muriel and Carol Osborne: *Amelia, My Courageous Sister.* Osborne Publishing, 1987
[4] A personal recollection of Amelia Earhart by Helen Schleman, April 13, 1975.
[5] *New York Herald Tribune*, July 8, 1937

Chapter Three: A Trio of School Spirits
[1] Mark Marimen; Personal Interviews and Research.

Chapter Four: The Spirit of Mercy
[1] Mark Marimen; Personal Interviews and Research.

Chapter Five: The Historic Haunts of Knox County

[1] *History of Indiana Vol. I* by Logan Esarey. Copyright 1918 by Logan Esary.

[2] *Indiana, A History* by William E. Wilson. Copyright 1966 by William E. Wilson, Indiana University Press.

[3] "A Haunted Tour of Knox County", available on the World Wide Web www.rking.vinu.edu/shake.htm

[4] "Ghost Rider Gallops into Haunting Legend" by Richard Day. *Valley Advance,* Vincennes, Indiana, October 27, 1981

Chapter Six: The Ghost Story That Never Was

[1] Mark Marimen; Personal Interviews and Research.

Chapter Seven: A Historic Haunted Mansion

[1] Mark Marimen, Personal interviews and research.

[2] *The James F. D. Lanier Mansion,* by Diana Lanier Smith, Copyright by Coleman Printing Co.

Chapter Eight: The World Largest Ghost Hunt

[1] Mark Marimen, Personal interviews and research.

Chapter Nine: Some Troublesome Hoosier Poltergeists

[1] Mark Marimen, Personal interviews and research.

[2] *Haunted Heartland* by Beth Scott and Michael Norman. Copyright 1985 by Michael Norman and Beth Scott.

Chapter Ten: Little Girl Lost

[1] Mark Marimen; Personal Interviews and Research.

Chapter Eleven: The Spirited Guests of French Lick Springs Resort

[1] "French Lick Grand Resort", available on the World Wide Web www.frenchlick.org

[2] Mark Marimen, Personal interviews and research

Postscript

Outside the wind whistles fitfully beneath the eves, reminding me that it is time to go to bed, and the fire in grate flickers in silent assent. Slowly, the spirits drawn up by the night and my imagination bow and begin to take their leave. A part of me is sorry to see them go, as they have been good company in these late hours. Yet I know they will return. The next dark night as the leaves skitter and the shadows draw near, they will return, like the old friends they are.

In the meantime, it is time for us to part once again. I hope that these stories have amused you, and perhaps even chilled you. More to the point, it is my hope that in their retelling they have woven their spell around you as they have around me. When the morning light comes shining through your windowpane you, like I, may be tempted to look back at them as the harmless musings of fable and myth, and perhaps they are.

However, the next time the shadows draw close, the night grows late, and your imagination begins to wander, don't be too shocked if, peering into the darkness, you find a few mutual friends, waiting to share a few hours with you. Don't be afraid. They are only as real as the flicker of firelight and the phantom wail of the wind. Instead, I hope you will sit back and enjoy their company.

And if you do… give them my best, won't you?

–MMW, September 15, 1999